VOICE
OF THE
CELTICS
JOHNNY MOST'S GREATEST CALLS

MIKE CAREY
WITH AUDIO CD BY
JAMIE MOST

www.SportsPublishingLLC.com

ISBN: 1-58261-850-X

Special thanks to Steve Lipofsky, Basketballphoto.com.

Publishers: Peter L. Bannon and Joseph J. Bannon Sr.
Senior managing editor: Susan M. Moyer
Acquisitions editor: Mike Pearson
Developmental editors: Kipp Wilfong and Erin Linden-Levy
Art director: K. Jeffrey Higgerson
Book design: Kenneth J. O'Brien
Dust jacket design: Kenneth J. O'Brien
Imaging: Kenneth J. O'Brien, Heidi Norsen and Dustin Hubbart
Vice president of sales and marketing: Kevin King
Media and promotions managers: Dan Waldinger (regional),
        Randy Fouts (national), Maurey Williamson (print)

Printed in the United States

Sports Publishing L.L.C.
804 North Neil Street
Champaign, IL 61820

Phone: 1-877-424-2665
Fax: 217-363-2073
Web site: www.SportsPublishingLLC.com

This book is dedicated to Mya, Jaden, Joshua, Sydney, Luc and those to follow, who never had the thrill of knowing their grandfather.

And to former Celtic Bob Brannum, one of the true "Good Guys."

Tommy Heinsohn was one of Johnny Most's closest friends and his narration on the CD provides a fitting backdrop for Johnny's famous calls. © Steve Lipofsky

Audio Contents

Contents

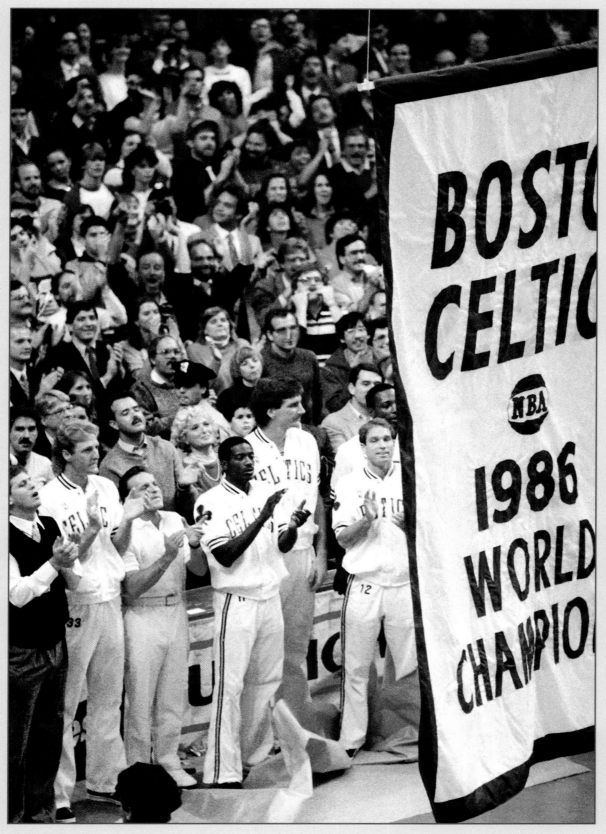

Acknowledgments

I would like to give a very special thank you to Tommy Heinsohn. His friendship with my father lives on forever. Thank you to all my friends at NBA Entertainment for all your help and support on this project: Adam Silver, Gregg Wink, Charlie Rosenzweig, Tom Carelli, David Denenberg, Joy Dellapina, John Hareas, Jared Franzreb, Dan Opallo, Scott Shniderman, and Mark Surhoff.

Thanks to the Boston Celtics and Jeff Twiss in particular, and to radio stations WBZ (AM) and WEEI for their enthusiastic support.

I would also like to acknowledge the efforts of a great many people who contributed in so many ways, as well as those organizations and institutions that showed immeasurable support when asked to help out. The common ground is a desire to see this tribute to Johnny Most completed in order that his legacy live on for generations to come.

Also, NBA commissioner David Stern, Tom Burke and the entire Walter Brown family, Mrs. Jim Pansullo, Gerald Henderson, Glenn Ordway, Gino Cappelletti, Rob Friedman, John Sykes, Ted Jordan, Peter Casey, Ethan Eichrodt, Deric "D-Dot" Angelettie, Jason Wolfe, Ray Flynn, Brian Wallace, the Grenert family, Lee Rubinstein, Dave Fried, my wife Chelsea, Rob Wallace, Brian Wick, Mike Porte, Gloria Contreras, Jason Camiolo, Bill Bosworth, Mike Allen, Richard Johnson, Don Makson, Boston College, Reid Oslin, Chris Cameron, the Boston Public Library, the Brannum family, and, of course, Margery Most, Rob Most and Andrea Gottschall, who understand the true meaning of family.

NBA audio archives provided by and copyright of NBA Entertainment. Audio also provided by: New England Sports Museum, Corbis in Motion, and the Most family archives (my dad had reel-to-reels stashed in his attic for many years).

I would also like to give a very special thanks to those private collectors who not only provided me with invaluable audio material, but also turned out to be a wealth of information: Ron Marshall, John Miley, Mel Simons, and Bill Fried.

A sincere thanks to producer Howie Sylvester, who had the foresight to save many of my dad's most memorable calls. Some audio segments have been edited for time and content. CD mastered at Audio Engine West, Phoenix, Arizona by Bobby Giammarco, mixing and editing engineer, who went way above and beyond. Narration recorded at Soundtrack, Boston, Massachusetts, by Kevin McLaughlin, recording engineer. Play-by-play calls and soundbites transferred at Audio Engine West, New York, New York, and Crazy Car Catalogue, Inc. New York, New York.

Celtics coach Red Auerbach is carried off the court by fans and players after Boston won the 1961 NBA championship. Johnny Most was behind the microphone for this and every other of the Celtics' 16 championships. AP/WWP

Preface

When *High Above Courtside: The Lost Memoirs of Johnny Most* was published a year ago, everyone who knew the legendary Celtics play-by-play announcer had a favorite "Most Moment." Former Boston players and coaches, opponents, referees, and colleagues all recalled in very specific details an example of why Johnny was the ultimate homer, the ultimate Celtics fan, and a one-of-a-kind broadcaster.

There is a reason why Most's classic calls of great moments in Celtics (and NBA) history are still used to introduce nationally televised games: Johnny's passion and enthusiasm for his team and for the game of basketball itself are unmatched even today—more than 11 years after he passed away.

Merely quoting Most's play-by-play descriptions throughout the years does not do justice to his knack of captivating his huge audience of Celtics fans. Johnny was an entertainer who used his amazing vocal range, his extreme emotionalism, along with his unique basketball vocabulary and use of the English language, to stir the imagination of his radio listeners. In the process, he managed to convince all of New England that Boston players never made a turnover, committed a foul, lost a fight or "legitimately" were outplayed in a single game.

Remarkably, the vast majority of Most's Celtics' calls were preserved on tape. The CD, which is the centerpiece of this book, was produced by Johnny's oldest son, Jamie. The various audio clips chosen for the disc are proof of why so many New England fans considered him to be their official spokesman and why the Boston players, coaches and management credit him for helping to create "Celtic Pride."

As veteran sportscaster Gil Santos said, "In Johnny's mind, the Celtics never lost a game. They just ran out of time." And Most did indeed believe Boston "deserved to be undefeated," as his audio calls will chronicle.

For longtime Celtics fans, Johnny's calls will bring to life numerous historical, nerve-wracking, sometimes humorous, memories. For those younger fans who may not have had the enjoyment of listening to Most root for Boston and belittle its enemies, the CD will not only entertain and serve as a Celtics history lesson but, more importantly, it also will provide an accurate portrait of sports' most colorful broadcaster.

Photo courtesy of the Most family

The Ultimate Celtics Fan
and Proud of It

or as long as Boston's NBA franchise exists, Johnny Most will be known as the "Voice of the Celtics." In the hearts of New England fans, Johnny Most, who passed away in 1993, earned that title, and no one else has the right to stake a claim to it.

It was Most who was behind the radio microphone for all 16 Celtics championship seasons; it was Most whose emotional play-by-play descriptions helped lure fans to the Boston Garden in the early '50s when the team was struggling to survive financially; it was Most whose classic calls of great moments in Celtics history are still utilized by the league as voice-overs to introduce nationally televised games; and it was Most—from "high above courtside"—who led the cheers as Red Auerbach, Walter Brown, John Havlicek, Bill Russell, Dave Cowens, Larry Bird, and other Celtics' Hall of Famers celebrated each crucial victory.

"I root for these guys on the air," Most once said. "I'd be a hypocrite if I didn't. I travel with them, I room with some of them, I eat my meals with them, I socialize with them. I'm around them constantly. They're my friends. How the hell can I be objective? To pretend I don't care if they win or lose would make me a complete phony. And that's something I am definitely not.

"Yes, I'm a homer, and I don't apologize for my broadcast style. The late Sam Cohen, sports editor of the *Record American*, gave me some great advice. He told me that if I didn't show emotion and enthusiasm on the air, then how could I possibly expect my audience to be excited about the Celtics? From that moment on, I just considered myself the one lucky Celtics fan who gets to tell all the other Celtics fans what's taking place on the court."

Talented Sean Grande, who has handled the Celtics broadcasting duties since 2001, fully realizes Most's place in the team's history. "I am not the voice of the Celtics. Johnny Most owns that distinction. I am just the current play-by-play announcer."

As Jim Karvellas, the highly respected 31-year radio and TV NBA play-by-play veteran, said, "Johnny may not have been the so-called 'perfect announcer,' an impartial suit-and-tie guy with a smooth delivery. But he was certainly the perfect announcer for all the fans of the Celtics. He was a beloved figure, not just in Boston but throughout New England."

In 1970, Karvellas, who was then the Baltimore Bullets radio and TV voice, was offered the job of handling the Celtics' play-by-play for WBZ-TV. "The station's general manager, Wyn Baker, gave me a very attractive offer. He told me to take a couple days, see the sights in Boston, and get a feel for just how much the fans care about the team," Karvellas recalled recently. "The more I talked to people, the more I realized that if I took the job, I probably wouldn't have much of an audience. Almost everyone told me that when the Celtics were on TV, they turned down the volume completely and listened to Johnny Most on WBZ radio.

"I went back to Wyn and told him, 'I really appreciate the offer, but this is Johnny Most's town. From the fans' viewpoint, the Celtics are Johnny's team. In my opinion, the TV job is a can't-win situation. I wish the guy who takes the job a lot of luck because it's going to take a miracle to get fans to break their habit of listening to Most while watching the games. I don't care how talented the guy might be.'"

A frustrated Baker knew Karvellas's assessment of the Boston fans' attitude was accurate. Even though the Celtics telecasts earned solid ratings, WBZ-TV had an unusually difficult task convincing advertisers that viewers would actually watch and listen to their commercials. "It's a tough sell—and it shouldn't be," Baker told Karvellas. "Too many advertisers are convinced the better way to spend their money is to let Most pitch their product on our radio side because a great number of TV viewers will hear their commercials, too."

Baker could have solved the problem by simulcasting the games, with Most handling both the TV and radio play-by-play. According to Johnny, Baker declined to even entertain the idea because "he thought I wasn't good-looking enough. Hell, to be blunt, he thought I was ugly. I certainly wasn't one of the new breed, the so-called pretty boys."

Three years later, WBZ, under new management, decided to utilize simulcasts. Most would announce the play-by-play, with Len Berman, a young and talented sportscaster, handling the color commentary. "For someone who was relatively new to the business, the experience was almost overwhelming," Berman, a five-time winner of New York's Sportscaster of the Year award, recalled recently. "Johnny was a great guy who was always giving me bits of advice. He made a conscious effort to be a mentor. However, it didn't take me long to realize that Johnny did not believe in 'discussions' between himself and his partner. He didn't run a democracy in the broadcast booth. When he paused, I knew I had four or five seconds—maximum—to make my observations. What made my analysis slightly more difficult was that there were times when I would have sworn Johnny and I were watching two different games. For instance, he'd be talking about the opponent's 'brutality and viciousness' underneath the boards and I'd have to mention that the Celtics held a 15-6 lead in rebounding. 'That just shows the Celtics' sheer desire,' Johnny would respond as he resumed his play-by-play."

The principal problem from the TV side of the simulcasts was that, there was no remote feed of the replays when the Most-Berman team were doing road games. "WBZ didn't want to spend the money it would cost," said Berman. "We couldn't even see the replays, yet I had to comment on them as if I was watching them. If we missed something interesting during the live action, then we obviously were going to miss it again on the replay." Johnny fought WBZ to spend the extra money for the remote feed but it was like talking to a wall. After the '73-'74 season, the grand experiment ended, with Most returning to his role handling radio play-by-play while Berman took over the TV announcing.

"It was the best thing that ever happened to Johnny. Television didn't do justice to his broadcasting ability," says Hall of Famer Tommy Heinsohn. "The job of a TV play-by-play man is simply to enhance the picture which viewers are seeing on the screen. On the radio, Johnny's words were the picture. His descriptions, his catchy phrases and nicknames, his emotionalism, his voice inflections, and, yes, even his embellishments painted the scene and allowed his listeners to use their imagination to view the game vividly in their minds. No one was better than Johnny Most at doing this—and Celtics fans knew it and appreciated his unique talent to make every game entertaining. It was classic radio, baby. When the game began, Johnny got strapped in, and off he went, full blast."

Legendary broadcaster Curt Gowdy (left) and Johnny Most appear on the court together during halftime in 1974, when the Celtics honored Johnny's 20 years as announcer. Photo courtesy of the Most family

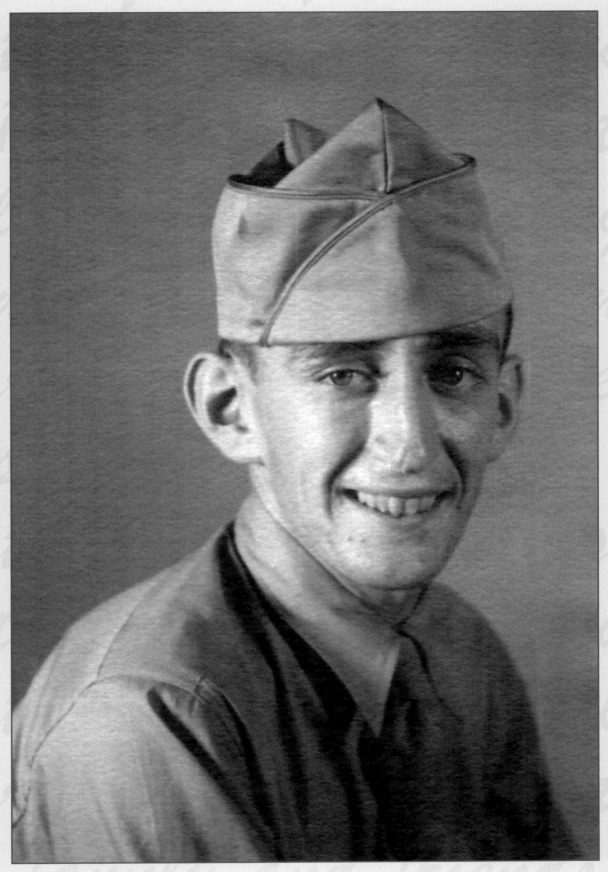

Photo courtesy of the Most family

Service to His Country
and a Message to His Parents

Before Johnny Most ever could venture into sportscasting, he was drafted into the Army in November of 1942, one month into his senior year at Brooklyn College. While training at Camp Breckenridge, Kentucky, prior to being ordered overseas, the 20-year-old recorded a heartfelt greeting to his parents, friends, and his cousin, Stu. Remarkably, that short message has been preserved. Johnny's soft-spoken, youthful voice provided a strong hint that he knew he was about to fight for his country.

Words did not come easily as he sought to reassure his family and friends that he was safe and well trained.

As World War II escalated, he spent his first year in the tank destroyers before transferring to the Army Air Corps where he served three years. Becoming a waist gunner and radio operator aboard a B-24 bomber, Most flew 28 raids across Europe and was awarded seven major battle stars, a Purple Heart, the Distinguished Flying Cross, the Air Medal and two Presidential Citations.

Johnny seldom talked about his World War II experiences. The memories, particularly the loss of many close friends, were too painful. As Celtics president Red Auerbach said, "Heroes don't go around taking bows for being heroes, but for those of us who knew his background, his combat experience was just one more reason to hold him in high regard."

Photo courtesy of the Most family

Johnny Most (bottom row, second from the left) and his B-24 crewmates in Canosa, Italy, in 1945. Photo courtesy of the Most family

Photo courtesy of the Most family

Johnny Most, age 27. Photo courtesy of the Most family

Paying His Dues

It was anything but instant stardom for Johnny Most when he decided to test the waters in the very competitive field of broadcasting while finishing his final few courses at Brooklyn College in 1945. During his nine months in the business, he landed a few bit parts in soap operas, worked on quiz shows, and handled acting, announcing and script writing for *FM Playhouse*. In between jobs, he attended more than a hundred auditions, with little success. "After expenses, I probably didn't make a dime. I lived with my parents, who were very generous and supportive."

Accepting a job as "assistant program director," Johnny moved to tiny Oil City, Pennsylvania, in February of 1946. His princely wages were $41.62 for a 58-hour work week. The job title may have sounded impressive, but Most did everything from being the morning newscaster/weatherman, to serving as the afternoon disc jockey, to hosting his first nightly sports show. Johnny loved the job—until the obnoxious station owner insulted one of his friends. Most immediately intervened, slugged the boss, and was canned on the spot. His first full-time radio job had lasted less than two months.

His first full-time sports position was at WNOC in Connecticut where he handled the morning and nightly ten-minute sportscasts, as well as announcing play-by-play of the Norwich Free Academy basketball games.

Slowly moving up the ladder, Most's next stop was at WVOS in New York's Catskill Mountain resort area. It was there he received the luckiest break of his career when 30-year-old sportscaster Marty Glickman happened to hear Johnny calling a Liberty High School basketball game while having a drink at Grossinger's. Glickman, who was both the Knicks and the New York Football Giants play-by-play announcer at the time, was impressed with Most's enthusiastic calls and arranged to meet the fledgling sportscaster that same afternoon.

"I couldn't believe that someone as famous as Marty Glickman wanted to talk to me. To this day, I absolutely idolize the guy," said Most in a 1983 interview. "Not only is he a great sportscaster, but he was a former world-class athlete. As an 18-year-old Syracuse University freshman, he had earned a spot on the heavily favored U.S. 400-yard relay team which was to compete at the 1936 Olympic Games in Berlin. However, at the last minute, (U.S. Olympic Committee Chairman) Avery Brundage, an out-and-out bigot and an admirer of Adolf Hitler, removed Marty and his teammate, Sam Stoller, for no other reason than they were Jewish. Brundage's cruel actions cost Marty his chance to win a gold medal.

"Despite the very personal injustice he suffered, Marty's love for sports competition didn't diminish. He returned to Syracuse, earning All-America honors as a tailback. After a short pro football and basketball career, he became the first jock-turned-sportscaster, the best there ever has been. ...By the time I first met him, he was regarded as the top play-by-play man and interviewer in the business."

Broadcaster Marty Glickman holds a photo of himself and Jesse Owens. Glickman, a world-class sprinter, was excluded from the 1936 Olympics in Berlin because he was Jewish. AP/WWP

Photo courtesy of the Most family

The pair's conversation lasted more than two hours. "I told Johnny he had a great voice and that his excitement for the game came through loud and clear to his audience," Glickman said. "As we talked, I could tell he had a tremendous knowledge of sports. I believed he could have a great future if he worked hard and met the right people. 'You've got all the basic skills; you've got a distinctive voice,' I told him. 'Now you have to make the right contacts.'"

With Glickman taking on the role of mentor, Johnny joined the New York Sportscasters' Association. "Once I got in, I never missed a meeting. In fact, I'd be the first to arrive and the last to leave," Most said. "This was, after all, a chance to be among my idols and listen to them exchange classic stories about athletes and broadcasters. I also got the opportunity to pick their brains about the tricks of the trade."

As Johnny molded his broadcasting style, he was influenced by four giants in the sportscasting industry—Ted Husing, Bill Stern, Mel Allen, and, above all, Glickman.

Husing took great pride in showing off his tremendous vocabulary and his knack for painting vivid pictures with his adjective-filled phrases. "I didn't like his choice of so many rarely used words and his rambling descriptions," Most said. "However, he had a deep voice, excellent knowledge of sports, and, most importantly, a style which was all his own. Because of him, I became very intent on developing my own method of describing a game. I wanted to be known as someone with originality rather than a guy who copied someone else's techniques."

Stern was opinionated, loud, cocky and controversial. "Howard Cossell was the poor man's Bill Stern," Johnny would say. "Howard copied Bill, but he didn't have half of Bill's talent. Nor did Cossell's imagination rival Stern's. If, for instance, Bill didn't know a player's background, he would just make up a couple of wild stories about the guy. He was a fast-thinker who believed that good fiction was more entertaining than dull facts. People claim I embellish and exaggerate. If I do—and I'm not admitting anything—I do so because of the influence of Stern's fascinating tall tales."

Johnny Most called Dodgers games from Ebbets Field in 1950.
Photo courtesy of the Most family

Photo courtesy of the Most family

Johnny's frequent use of nicknames for players, coaches and even referees was largely due to the influence of Yankee broadcaster Mel Allen. "As someone who grew up listening to Mel, I found it clever when he referred to shortstop Phil Rizzuto as 'The Little Scooter,' Joe DiMaggio as 'Joltin' Joe' and Mickey Mantle as 'The Mick.' Even Allen's description of a home run as a 'Ballantine Blast' was, in my opinion, colorful and inventive," said Most. "I didn't really use nicknames until I started broadcasting the Celtics. Fans would tell me they liked some of the ones I came up with, so I just kept inventing new ones through the years."

From Glickman, Johnny learned the basics of his delivery. "Marty spoke in short, rapid-fire sentences or sentence fragments. He used just enough words to accurately describe the action. Marty told me, 'If you try to tell your audience every little thing that's happening during a game, you'll be lost and so will your audience. Keep your eyes focused on the key action.'"

Glickman used his voice to create an emotionally charged broadcast. He seldom became emotional, but he knew how to quickly raise or lower his vocal tones to evoke tension, surprise, disappointment or anger from his listeners. No one, in Johnny's opinion, was better.

Several years after his initial meeting with Glickman, Johnny teamed up with Kevin Kennedy to host a nightly sports talk show on WFDR in New York City. "The listeners thought we hated each other," said Most. "We'd stage heated arguments. We'd take the most controversial stands you can imagine just to draw the listeners' interest. We weren't above playing pranks on the air. When we'd report the scores and highlights of games, we'd make up names just to see if the audience would catch us. For instance, I'd say, 'The Indians beat the White Sox, 3-2,' and Kevin would add, 'on a 450-foot homer by George Fink.' We both knew there was no such player as George Fink but we were impish enough to see if we could sneak it by. ...We usually succeeded."

Johnny's first "big-time" job was as broadcaster for the newly created Brooklyn Dodgers Radio Network. He had spotted an ad for the job in the *Radio Daily* and sent in a resume. He was notified by mail that he, along with more than 300 other applicants, would be considered for the position. Most immediately dismissed his chances of being hired. "You never know," Glickman told him. "They may want someone relatively new. They may not give a damn about experience. You've got the talent. I see it. Maybe they will, too."

A month and a half later, Johnny received a phone call from Jim Stevenson, who was in charge of establishing the Dodger Radio Network. "(Team owner) Branch Rickey says the job is yours if you want it," Stevenson said.

"I know this is a joke," Johnny replied. "Which wiseass put you up to this?"

"Well," answered Stevenson, "the wiseass is Branch Rickey, and the job is really yours if you want it."

Needless to say, Johnny accepted the job "faster than you could say Jack Robinson." In April of 1950, he officially became radio network voice of the "Boys of Summer." Most broadcast all the home games live from Brooklyn's Ebbets Field. Because of a tight budget, the away games were "recreated" in a small studio in New York City. "All I had to work with was the Western Union ticker tape, which gave the ball-and-strike counts and a brief description of each play. As an example, if Duke Snider hit a liner to center on which Phillies star Richie Ashburn made a diving one-handed catch, all that the ticker tape would reveal was: 'SNIDER FLIES OUT ON 3-2 COUNT. TWO OUTS. DODGER SIXTH INNING.' So, I was forced to use my imagination. I'd have to 'fill in the blanks' by describing a play as my mind saw it happening. At the same time, I'd use sound effects of crowd noise as background to give the audience the impression I was actually at the game."

It was definitely a challenge, but one Johnny loved. "Here I was sitting in this dark, dirty little room, pretending I was watching a major league game. I literally had to bring every away game to life by making up a million details about what was taking place on a baseball diamond I couldn't see," he said. "The biggest problem was when the Western Union ticker tape broke down. Then I had to stall for time. I'd tell the audience about an imaginary fight between the players. If the tape still wasn't working, I'd invent a long and heated argument between a manager and an ump. I had a list of about 20 stall tactics to use if necessary."

One afternoon in the fall of '51, Johnny received an emergency call from WMGM, which carried the Knicks games. Marty Glickman and his color commentator, Bert Lee Jr., were stranded by a blizzard and would not be able to get to New York in time to broadcast the Knicks game that night. The caller said Glickman had recommended Most. "Is there any chance you can fill in?" the man asked Johnny. "I'm on my way," replied the 28-year-old sportscaster. "I'll be there in 30 minutes."

"Johnny was tremendous," said Glickman. "People at the radio station all kidded me that he was better than I was. You know, people said I helped Johnny's career by getting him jobs. The truth is Johnny's talent helped him get jobs. I helped him because he was so gifted, not because I did him any favors. He won the Dodgers job because of his skills. He beat out hundreds of applicants. Sure, I recommended him to fill in for me for one game with the Knicks. But it was his professionalism in

Johnny Most and his family stand on the court at Boston Garden. Photo courtesy of the Most family

doing that one game which earned him the respect of the WMGM bosses and the New York fans."

Two months later WMGM asked Johnny to become Glickman's full-time color man because Lee was being drafted into the Army. "This was my dream job. I was only 28 years old, working with my idol," said Most. "I would have done it for free. Marty gave me a lot of freedom on the air and a lot of advice off the air. He let me handle the postgame interviews. He made it clear from the start that we were partners. He made sure I had a prominent role on every broadcast."

"I wasn't being charitable to John," said Glickman. "I didn't have to carry him. He was already a pro. He knew my style and I knew his. It was a partnership that just clicked."

When Lee was discharged from the Army two years later, Johnny quit the Knicks job even though team president Ned Irish urged WMGM to retain Most as Glickman's sidekick. Fortunately for Most, the Boston Celtics were looking for a play-by-play man to replace Curt Gowdy, who was leaving to broadcast the Red Sox, as well as announce some games for national TV.

Glickman immediately phoned Celtics coach Red Auerbach to urge him to hire Johnny. "Red was a good friend of mine. He had known Johnny for several years. He knew Johnny was good. I didn't have to sell him on the idea," Glickman said years later. "Red told me not to worry. If the decision was up to him, Johnny would

Johnny Most joins the Celtics for a team photo in 1961. He is seated in the middle row on the far right. Photo courtesy of the Most family

get the job. However, he said he'd have to get (Celtics owner) Walter Brown's approval."

When Johnny called Auerbach a few hours later to inquire about the opening, Red gave Johnny a scare. "Why didn't you call me sooner? The auditions have already begun. We've already picked five talented guys to compete," he said. Then Auerbach paused for a second and added, "But I guess we can make it six."

For his audition, Johnny was assigned the job of broadcasting a Knicks-Celtics exhibition game in New Haven, Connecticut. After the game, Auerbach put in a call to Celtics owner Walter Brown. "Well, what did you think of that Most guy?" Auerbach asked Brown as Johnny stood next to Red.

"I loved him," said Brown. "But will a Boston audience accept a New Yorker as our play-by-play man?"

"Why wouldn't they?" Red replied. "I'm from New York and they haven't run me out of town yet."

"OK, then Most has got the job 'cause he's the guy I want," Brown said. "You might as well cancel the rest of the auditions and let him finish out the rest of the exhibition schedule."

Auerbach hung up the phone and informed Johnny, "Well, it's all set. Walter talked me into it. You've got the job."

Photo courtesy of the Most family

Introducing
Himself to Celtics Fans

Before his regular-season debut in 1953 as the Celtics broadcaster, Johnny Most formulated his opening lines. He wanted to compose a few quick, simple and friendly sentences which would set the stage for each game. As he sat in the first row of the Boston Garden balcony, he wrote down some thoughts. The phrase "high above courtside" came to his mind.

"I just scribbled those words down. It took me just a minute or so to come up with an introduction which would basically stay the same for 37 years," Most said. "The only times I changed it just a little was when we were on the road and I'd be at courtside instead of broadcasting from upstairs."

Even today, longtime Boston fans can recite Johnny's "intro" by heart: "Hi there, everybody. This is Johnny Most, high above courtside at the Boston Garden, where the Boston Celtics and the (opponent's name) prepare to do basketball battle."

Lakers broadcaster Chick Hearns (left) and Johnny Most engage in a war of words before their teams do "basketball battle." © Steve Lipofsky

Johnny's Broadcasting Basics

When Johnny Most took over for popular and knowledgeable Curt Gowdy, he knew it would take awhile for the fans of New England to accept him as the Celtics' play-by-play announcer. Gowdy was known for his casual, straight-forward broadcasting technique. It is often said that when fans listened to Gowdy, it was as if he were sitting in their living rooms simply chatting about the action taking place on the court. "I had the privilege of working with Curt a couple of times during my first year with the Celtics," Johnny said. "He was just so relaxed, so smooth. It came naturally to him."

For the first year, Most attempted to be an objective play-by-play man. He was not satisfied with his performance. "I was trying to be 'too professional.' I had no personality, no flair. I was just going through the motions. My broadcasts were very stiff, very matter-of-fact," he admitted.

Then *Record American* sports editor Sammy Cohen gave Most a fatherly lecture. "You've got to become a fan yourself if you're going to be appreciated by the people in this town," the veteran newspaperman said. "Show your emotions. Let the audience know that you want to see the Celtics win, just like they do."

It made sense to Most, who desperately wanted to develop his own unique style. "I made up my mind that I was going to root like hell for Boston, just like the fans who were listening to me," he said. "I was going to be one of them. I was going to be the self-appointed president of the Celtics fan club."

On the air, Johnny would relentlessly attack the opposition and the referees for their underhanded tactics while lauding the Boston players for their heroism in the face of such unfair adversity. New England fans fell in love with Most's colorful, biased broadcasts and his total loyalty to Red Auerbach's fearless band of players.

"There were other announcers who openly rooted for their teams. Bob Prince, with the Pirates, and Harry Caray, broadcasting the Cubs, were two of the best known," Gowdy said. "But when Johnny did a Celtics game, he might as well have been wearing a Celtics jersey and sitting next to Auerbach."

Most didn't believe in any so-called set of broadcasting rules.

"Hell, everyone says I broke all the rules of broadcasting. And I'm sure I came close," Johnny said in a 1986 interview. "However, the one rule I always stuck to

Johnny Most does a postgame interview in the Celtics locker room.
Photo courtesy of the Most family

was to be myself on the air. If you try to imitate someone else, you will always be a second-rate broadcaster. Too many play-by-play guys are clones. They all sound alike. And they come across as phonies.

"If you're excitable, it's perfectly okay to be that way. On the other hand, if you're trying to force excitement in your voice, it won't work. Too many broadcasters today yell and scream about every halfway decent play. It's artificial—and the listeners are smart enough to realize it. Fans can spot a faker a mile away."

Most also didn't believe in reciting statistics a hundred times a game. "Far too many broadcasters drop in little stats every chance they get. They use statistics to cover up their own lack of knowledge about the game and the players. Who really cares if a player has hit three of eight shots? Who gives a damn if a player has two fouls early in the third quarter? Those stats are all but meaningless. A good broadcaster talks about why a team is or isn't having success, why a player is having a good game. A good broadcaster talks about strategy, not statistics.

As former Celtic Rick Weitzman, who was Most's color commentator for five years, said, "Johnny didn't know stats, but he sure knew the game of basketball. When I first became his partner, he told me what he expected from me. 'You're the expert,

Rick. Talk to the audience about what the Celtics are trying to do and why it's effective or why it isn't. Don't get too technical and don't talk down to the audience,' he told me. 'Just relax, be yourself, and you'll do great.' Johnny really treated me well, but I got a kick out of him telling me to relax. I mean he was a guy who smoked three packs of cigarettes a game because he was so nervous about whether the Celtics would win."

Johnny believed that the few stats which did matter were the score, the time remaining on the 24-second clock, and the time remaining in each quarter. "Many fans don't listen to the game from start to finish," he said. "You have to give scoring updates every couple of minutes because there are people out there who have just turned on the radio. Above everything else, they want to know who's winning and by how many points.

"In my opinion, the most important aspect of the game to emphasize is matchups. It's the individual battles which usually tell most of the story about strategy. I usually can tell how the game will be decided just by analyzing matchups. If you know which team the matchups favor, you'll be better prepared when it comes to keeping up with the play-by-play. That's been my experience, at least."

Johnny Most smiles from his broadcasting position in Philadelphia in 1974.
Photo courtesy of the Most family

Maurice Stokes (left) and Norm Drucker. Photo courtesy of Norm Drucker

Johnny's All-Star Game Call
January 15, 1957

The Year was 1951. College point-shaving scandals had all but destroyed the future of basketball. Attendance was poor at the college level and absolutely dismal at the pro games. The NBA was only five years old. It had gone from 17 teams in '49-'50 to just 11 because of financial difficulties.

Celtics owner Walter Brown proposed that the league hold an annual All-Star game. His suggestion was scoffed at by virtually every other team. Even Maurice Podoloff, the league's commissioner, was dead set against the idea. An All-Star game, the commissioner argued, would be a financial flop. "Besides," said Podoloff, "when no one shows up to watch, it will be sending a message that no one takes pro basketball seriously."

But a stubborn Brown refused to abandon his proposal. "If the league holds the game in Boston, I'll cover any losses and I'll pay for all the expenses," he told the other owners. "We've got a good product. If any owner doesn't believe that, he should fold his team right now."

Reluctantly, the team owners allowed Brown to stage the event. To the amazement of the entire league, the first annual All-Star game drew 10,094 spectators and was praised by the media as a stroke of marketing genius.

In January 15, 1957, Boston hosted the seventh NBA All-Star game. Handling both the national and local radio play-by-play was none other than Johnny Most.

Much to the surprise of his audience, Johnny handled the play-by-play in a less subjective manner than usual. As you will hear, Most uncharacteristically gave his best attempt at calling it straight as the East beat the West, 109-97.

"Each player, no matter what team they played for, was a star," he explained afterward. "It wouldn't have been fair for me to root for one guy over another, although I definitely became a little bit more excited when a Celtic player, particularly Cousy, who was the game's MVP, made an outstanding play. In general, though, I toned it down on purpose—just for this one game."

Ironically, the one All-Star player who received the most accolades from Johnny during that game was not a Celtic. "I commented a great deal about the pure athleticism of former Rookie of the Year Maurice Stokes, a forward who played for the Rochester Royals," Johnny recalled. "He was a youngster, just 24 years old, but he could play every position like a veteran. He had that much poise and skill. In that All-Star game he had 19 points, 12 rebounds, and seven assists. Defensively, he was brilliant in that game.

"Tragically, Stokes was struck down by encephalitis the following season. The disease left him paralyzed for 12 years before it ultimately claimed his life in 1970. He was an All-Star each of his three NBA seasons, and, in my opinion was one of the top five players in the league. His only weakness was outside shooting, but there's no doubt in my mind he would have improved quickly because Maurice had a tremendous work ethic. His quickness, passing ability and court awareness were just unbelievable. When I first saw Magic Johnson play, it brought back memories of Maurice. You have to understand that Stokes was 6'7" and weighed 240 pounds. He could handle the ball like a point guard and rebound like a center. It was impossible not to rave about his abilities and potential. I'll always wonder just how great he might have become."

Maurice Stokes (left) and Jack Twyman, Stokes's teammate and legal guardian, hold their Philadelphia Sports Writers Association Awards for "Most Courageous Athlete" in 1962. AP/WWP

Johnny Most wasn't the only one who had a problem with referee Sid Borgia's (left) calls. Hal Tyson holds back Syracuse coach Paul Seymour in 1960. AP/WWP

Fighting for the Celtics—Right From the Start

When Johnny Most accepted the job as Boston's broadcaster, he didn't waste any time becoming defender of the green and white and verbal tormentor of opposition players and coaches, as well as referees.

During his first year behind the microphone, Johnny directed a 20-second tongue lashing towards referee Sid Borgia during a playoff game in St. Louis. "I was listening to the game," recalled Curt Gowdy. "Borgia called a charge against Bob Cousy. He was so close to Most's courtside seat that I could hear his whistle. Johnny immediately reacted by yelling, 'That's ridiculous. That's positively outrageous. It was an obvious blocking foul. ...That's the worst call I've ever seen. That official is either blind, incompetent, or crooked.' I nearly fell off my chair from shock. I had never heard a broadcaster come close to criticizing a ref with those kind of words."

(Borgia heard about Most's comments and almost filed a lawsuit.)

There also were occasions when Johnny went far beyond mere verbal sparring with "the enemy." For instance, following a 1954 Celtics-Hawks game which ended in a 20-minute brawl, St. Louis owner Ben Kerner approached Most and began to berate the Celtic players, Red Auerbach, and Johnny himself. "Kerner's choice of four-letter words finally got to me," Most said. "I just dropped my radio equipment and whacked him one right in the puss. Got him good, too."

Four years later, Kerner attempted to harass Johnny by selling his regular broadcasting seat on press row to a fan, forcing Most to call the game from the end of the Celtics bench. "It was the weirdest situation I ever encountered. I was sitting next to Gene Conley, who was a very funny guy," Johnny recalled. "Gene would listen in on my calls and start making little jokes about the Hawks' players. He was so humorous that I started handing him the microphone when he had something to say. The only time he wasn't my color commentator that day was when Red told him to go into the game to give Bill Russell a breather."

The NBA's fiercest rivalry during Most's first few years was Syracuse versus Boston. In '54, the Celtics played a particularly physical game against the Nats at the Garden in the playoffs. With less than ten seconds remaining in regulation, Schayes hit a layup to tie the score. He then batted the ball out of bounds to prevent the Celtics from inbounding the ball quickly. However, Boston ballboy Ray Flynn—the same Ray Flynn who went on to be an NIT MVP and later, mayor of Boston—intercepted the ball and immediately flipped it to a Celtic, who threw a long upcourt pass. It set up an easy Celtics layup, which turned out to be the game winner.

The Celtics' first "enforcer," Bob Brannum, shoves a Syracuse defender.
Photo courtesy of the Brannum family

Nats coach Al Cervi and 220-pound forward Wally Osterkorn witnessed the play and ran over to the 12-year-old Flynn and began to yell at him.

In the broadcast booth, Most started screaming, "They're trying to attack the young kid. Now they're twisting another ballboy's (John "Engine" Horan) arm. This is a disgrace. These bullies want to physically harm two young ballboys. Those poor kids are defenseless against two grown men."

As soon as the game ended, Johnny made a passionate plea to his audience: "I very rarely make a request, but I'm imploring you to come up to Syracuse for the next game. Bring some form of weapon for self-protection because you'll probably need it. You're going to do a lot of things in your life which won't be as meaningful as going to Syracuse to help keep our players safe from the crude, unruly mob of people who call themselves basketball fans. These people buy a ticket to the game and think the ticket entitles them to be participants on the court. I'm telling you the truth. The

Celtics need your help up there in the nut house they call the War Memorial Auditorium."

Then Johnny headed to the Boston locker room where he sought out the hero of the day, young Raymond Flynn. "Well, son, you've just won your first game for the Celtics," the smiling Most said. "That was a hell of a job you did."

Before the next game in Syracuse, the Nats handed out 5,000 cardboard hatchets to their fans. Each one had a handwritten inscription on the hatchet which read: BRANNUM "THE HATCHET MAN" (IN BOSTON). Just as the tipoff was about to take place, the majority of those 5,000 hatchets were thrown onto the court. Bob Brannum, who relished his reputation as an enforcer, scrambled around the court collecting as many of them as he could. "They'll make great souvenirs," he said after the game. "I'm going to give them to my friends and put one on top of my locker. I guess this shows that I'm doing my job. My thanks to the good people of Syracuse for honoring me."

"During the first half, I had a major problem," Most said. "Some drunk in the row behind me was yelling nonstop at Brannum. The guy was such an obnoxious loud-mouth that his slurred comments could distinctly be heard on the air. During a timeout, I finally told the guy to "kindly shut up." He staggered towards me and started to throw a punch. I ducked and then landed an uppercut, which opened up a cut on his lower lip. The security people witnessed the whole incident—and did absolutely nothing. (That was par for the course in Syracuse.) My broadcast, however, went along smoothly from that point because the heckler's lip was so swollen he couldn't talk, much less yell. He just sat there in a complete stupor."

Whenever Brannum spotted Johnny in a heated confrontation, he silently provided back-up. "I'd just walk up behind John, point a warning finger at the heckler or hecklers, and then make a fist," he said. "That's usually all it took to put the trou-blemakers back in their seats and allow Johnny to broadcast the game without any more interruptions."

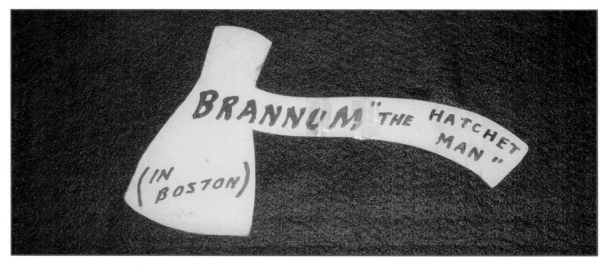

Photo courtesy of the Brannum family

Rookie center Bill Russell (6) was instrumental in the Celtics' 1957 championship.
AP/WWP

That Championship Feeling
April 13, 1957

For Johnny Most's first three seasons, the Celtics had little postseason success, failing to win even a single division title. However, when Red Auerbach drafted Holy Cross forward Tommy Heinsohn and traded for the rights to 6'9" Bill Russell of the University of San Francisco, the Celtics were transformed into the dominating force of the Eastern Division.

Although Russell was unavailable until late December because he was starring for the '56 U.S. Olympic team, Heinsohn's 20 points and 11 rebounds a game helped Boston jump out to a six-game lead in the East. "I had (Bob) Cousy setting me up for easy shots on the fastbreak and (Bill) Sharman, along with (Frank) Ramsey spreading the defense with their outside jumpers," said Heinsohn, who would go on to win Rookie of the Year honors.

When Russell made his pro debut on December 22, grabbing 16 rebounds as the Celtics overcame a 16-point fourth-quarter deficit, a hoarse Johnny Most told his audience this edition of the Celtics was destined for a run at the NBA championship. "You have to forgive me for losing my voice," he said, "but we've just witnessed the birth of a star and the start of a new era in Boston history...I just saw (St. Louis All-Star forward) Bob Pettit shaking his head in total disgust—and that's a great sight for every Celtics fan."

The Celtics finished the regular season with a league-best 44-28 record and then swept the Eastern finals, 3-0, over the hated Nationals. "Sweet revenge, baby," said Most after Boston won by 15 at War Memorial Auditorium in Game 2. "The Syracuse fans are booing their own team, not us. They're crying in their beer."

The seven-game finals against St. Louis was, in Johnny's words, an all-out war, especially after the Hawks won the opener in Boston as Pettit poured in 34 points in a 125-123 overtime win.

Before Game 3, Red Auerbach and Johnny's old sparring partner, Ben Kerner, engaged in a one-sided fistfight, with Red landing a good right-handed hook while a scared-looking Kerner retaliated with a feeble slap. "I could have knocked the guy out, except the SOB would have sued me," Auerbach told referee Norm Drucker.

The physical series went the full seven games. Three hours before the championship game tipoff at the Boston Garden, Most was pacing the hallway, drinking some coffee and checking to make sure he had an ample supply of cigarettes. "After three years of watching this team fall short, of seeing my friends suffer so much frustration, I was the most nervous I had ever been before any game I had worked," Johnny said. "I made sure I had a pack of English Ovals in every pocket and an emergency pack in my briefcase. I didn't want to run out of smokes."

As things turned out, Johnny had to "bum" more cigarettes because the game wouldn't be decided until a second overtime. "I thought we were in some real trouble because nothing was dropping for (the starting backcourt of) Bob Cousy and Bill Sharman," said Most. "They were our two veteran leaders and they shot only five for 40 in the game. On any other team, that would mean utter disaster."

But Heinsohn's all-around effort (37 points and 23 rebounds), Russell's rebounding and shot blocking, and Ramsey's outside baskets allowed Boston to match the Hawks basket for basket.

In fact, Boston had a chance to win in regulation, but Pettit's two free throws with seven seconds remaining tied the score at 103-103 and forced an overtime. In that first OT, Boston again had an opportunity to claim the championship but a last-second shot by Sharman was off-target, forcing overtime number two.

"I was soaked in sweat and my voice was cracking. This was the most emotionally draining game I had ever announced," Johnny said afterward. "Then we finally forced a crucial St. Louis mistake." After Ramsey put Boston ahead by three with a jumper, Hawks forward Alex Hannum, pressured by a double-team, was called for traveling with eight seconds left. When Jungle Jim Loscutoff hit a free throw with one second left, the Celtics had all but secured their first NBA title, leading 125-123. The ensuing Hawks' desperation upcourt inbounds pass hit the backboard and bounced into the hands of pettit. The Hawks forward's jumper from 10 feet beat the buzzer but failed to clear the rim. An elated Most began to describe the on-the-court celebration. "All I could say was, 'It's all over. It's over.' Then the Garden fans swarmed the players. It was just a tremendous way for Boston to win its first championship."

Marty Glickman was in attendance, just two seats away from his former Knicks broadcasting partner. "Johnny did an incredible job," he recalled years later. "With that quick delivery of his and the unique phrases he used in the play-by-play, the listeners couldn't help but be excited. Of course, there was also that incredible voice of his. It was such an historic event—and I know there isn't anybody who could have done a better job at providing such an emotional account of it."

Walter Brown (far left) and the Celtics celebrate the 1957 Eastern Division championship. Red Auerbach is in the center with his trademark cigar. AP/WWP

All-Star MVP Ed Macauley (22) and East teammate Bob Cousy (14) had Celtics owner Walter Brown to thank for the creation of the NBA All-Star game in 1951, held in Boston Garden. Basketball Hall of Fame/NBAE/Getty Images

Walter Brown—No. 1 in Johnny's Mind

The fate of Boston's NBA franchise was very much in doubt when Johnny Most accepted the offer to become the Celtics' play-by-play announcer in 1953. Only one man, team owner Walter Brown, was totally convinced that coach Red Auerbach and his players could succeed in drawing enough fans to at least pay the bills and break even.

"Walter Brown poured his heart and his soul into making the Celtics a winner, both on the court and as a business venture," said Johnny. "He gave a hundred percent effort every single day. He expected the same work ethic from each of his employees. Times were tough. There were months when Walter couldn't meet expenses. His own family even begged him to sell the franchise or just fold it. Things were that bad in the early '50s. It wasn't uncommon for the team to draw less than 2,000 fans for games. The team would usually announce that attendance was 3,000 or a little better, but, in reality, those figures were pure fiction. There was no way the Celtics were making money."

Brown, however, was stubborn. Despite the team's constant debts, he found ways to keep the Celtics alive. "Walter had a great reputation because he had been successful running both the Boston Arena and the Boston Garden. The business community knew he was a man of his word. Because he was such an honest person and a true gentleman, almost every creditor accepted Walter's personal guarantee that they would eventually be paid in full," said Most. "Everyone who worked for him knew how much he loved the team and how much he cared about his employees. He had their total respect.

"I can tell you there were times when the payroll couldn't be met. The first salary Walter Brown eliminated was his own. Then he'd ask some of his employees, including Red, if they could give him an extra couple of weeks or so to pay them. No one complained. Somehow, some way, he always managed to keep things afloat. I know that he mortgaged his house. I also believe he borrowed at least a hundred thousand dollars more at his own personal risk."

Despite Brown's own financial problems, he was always concerned with making sure his employees' lives were going well. "You have to remember that players didn't make that much money in the early years of the league," Johnny said. "Walter Brown, as well as Red, would help them find jobs for the summer. If Walter found out that a player or an office worker was in need of money, he'd mail them a check and enclose a short note. He helped me out a couple times without my asking, so I know from personal experience how caring a person he was."

Things started looking up for the Celtics when Walter Brown (left) signed Bill Russell (right) in 1956. Co-owner Lou Pieri looks over Russell's shoulder as he reads the fine print. Sporting News/Getty Images

Brown wasn't quite perfect, though. "Walter wore his heart on his sleeve," Most said. "He had a quick fuse at times. He'd get angry when a player had a bad game and would make a negative comment to the media. However, the next day he'd tell the writers to 'say something good' about the very player he had criticized because he felt badly about his negative remarks. He also had his share of disagreements with Red, such as when he wanted to draft Cousy and Auerbach didn't. Still, he respected Red and always would quickly patch things up. He just wanted his team to win so badly that he occasionally would vent his frustrations."

When the Celtics' fortunes changed with the acquisition of Russell and the drafting of Heinsohn in 1956, Brown gradually began to recoup all his monetary losses. "He had always been so proud of this team and all the people who worked for him," said Johnny. "Now he had the opportunity to enjoy the rewards of all the risks he had

George McKeon and George Steinbrenner, principal stockholders in the Cleveland professional basketball team, pose with some NBA officials after Cleveland was voted into the NBA on July 10, 1962. From left: McKeon, Steinbrenner, Dan Biasone (Syracuse Nationals president), Walter Brown (Boston Celtics president), Ned Irish (New York Knickerbockers president), and Ben Kerner (St. Louis Hawks president).
AP/WWP

taken. Still, he worked 15-hour days. The dynasty years were great times for Walter, although he was always nervous and high-strung. He didn't like being in the spotlight, even following a championship win. He'd be in the locker room, standing against a wall all by himself watching everyone else celebrate. That was Walter's true joy, seeing the happiness of his 'Celtics family.' Because of Walter and Red, that phrase—Celtics family—will always have true meaning."

(In Johnny's interview with the Celtics owner, there's no mistaking Brown's humility and devotion to the team he founded.)

At age 59, Brown suffered a fatal heart attack on September 7, 1964. Johnny was devastated. "I thought the guy, with all his energy, would live to be 100," Johnny said. "He was a big man with a big heart, so trusted and admired by everyone who ever dealt with him. He was a big shot who didn't want to be one. I thought of him as a great person, not simply as a good boss. And in an instant he was gone. I couldn't believe it.

"When the Celtics raised the number '1' to the Garden rafters in Walter's honor a month after his death, the moving ceremony was a fitting tribute to the man who was solely responsible for enabling this team to survive financially and go on to become sport's greatest franchise. As the banner was being hoisted, I started to describe the atmosphere, but I had to stop because I was too choked up. As much as any player, Walter Brown was both a hero and friend to me."

© Steve Lipofsky

Bill Russell (6) outreaches Philadelphia's Wilt Chamberlain (13) to control the rebound. AP/WWP

The Genius
of Bill Russell

*J*ohnny didn't like to use the phrase "the greatest" to describe any Celtic. However, he came close to using that description whenever he would talk about the play of Bill Russell.

In Most's opinion, Russell was clearly a better center than Wilt Chamberlain. "Wilt was so caught up with his own personal achievements; Russ had but one goal, to help win games and championships," said Johnny. "Bill couldn't hit an open eight-foot jumper to save his life, yet he provided the spark for the almost unstoppable Celtics' fastbreak. Chamberlain cared about getting his points; Russell was concerned about setting up his teammates for their points. The difference between Wilt's mentality and Russell's was like night and day.

"Russell changed how the game of basketball was played with his defensive genius—the rebounding, the quick outlet passes to (Bob) Cousy, and especially the blocked shot. He made an art out of using smart, hard-nosed defense to create easy offensive plays. There were more than a few guys around the NBA who could leap higher than the 6'9" Russell but not a single one of them could hold Bill's jock strap when it came to timing a jump or anticipating where a rebound would fall. It was almost a science for the guy."

As for shot blocking, Russell had the unique skill of swatting the ball accurately to a teammate. "He not only kept the ball in play and got it to a teammate, but nine out of ten times Russell would be able to direct the block to a guard, usually Cousy or KC (Jones). That would set up the fastbreak," said Johnny. "Yes, Wilt had the height advantage, the strength advantage. What he didn't possess was Russell's brain power."

"Rapid Robert" Cousy drives around New York's Bob McNeill for a layup.
Larry C. Morris/New York Times Co./Getty Images

The Magic Touch
of Bob Cousy

When Johnny Most first began broadcasting the Celtics, he quickly discovered he was going to have one not-so-slight problem calling the game.

"My play-by-play had to keep up with Bob Cousy," he said. And that was no easy task because no one, including his teammates, was ever quite sure what Cousy would do with the ball. All they knew was if they ran at full speed and got open, Cousy would invent a pass that would leave them with an easy shot. I've got to admit that there were times when he caught me so off guard that I was literally stuttering, searching for words to describe how he had just completely fooled an entire defense with one of his spontaneous passes or with his dribbling ability.

"It took time to expect the unexpected because for 'Rapid Robert,' as I called him, there was no such thing as an impossible pass. When he had the ball, I was forced to pick up the pace of my delivery. I wasn't sure what was going to happen. All I knew was that the odds were Cousy would create something spectacular."

Cousy's repertoire was seemingly endless. There were his behind-the-back tosses to streaking teammates, his no-look flips, the perfectly timed bounce passes, which often went through a defender's legs, and his backwards taps which came after he made a spin move towards the basket. He'd ad-lib as he sized up the opponent's defense.

"Bob's skills became even more effective when Russell joined the team," said Johnny. With Russ dominating the boards and immediately finding Cousy with the outlet pass, the Celtics almost always would have at least a one- or two-man advantage on the break. The other team would be scrambling to get back on defense as Cousy masterminded the offense. It was, in Most's words, like taking candy from a baby.

"The Celtics would end up with a string of easy baskets," said Johnny, "and the 24-second clock would usually tick off only six or seven seconds on Boston's possessions."

Creating shot opportunities for himself was Cousy's least favorite option, even though he averaged over 18 points a game for his career. If the defense dropped off him, anticipating he was going to pass, then the Boston playmaker would occasionally take a pull-up, simply to keep the opponents honest. If no one was open on the break, then he'd drive toward the basket and either use a running right-handed hook shot or attempt a layup. Cousy knew that if he missed, Russell, running at full speed and trailing him, would be in position to snatch the rebound and go up for an uncontested layup.

"The Cousy years were fun to watch and a bit of a challenge to broadcast," Most said. "What also made the Celtics so effective was that Cousy's passing game made everyone on the team realize that if they moved the ball around quickly, someone would have to be open. It wasn't unusual to see three or even four guys touch the ball on a possession which took less than ten seconds to complete."

It's been well documented that Auerbach originally didn't want Cousy, whose rights were obtained by Boston only because the Celtics lost a coin flip in a 1951 dispersal draft. However, "The Cooz" quickly earned Auerbach's respect.

"It didn't take Red long to realize that Bob's flashy style wasn't merely 'showboating.' Every tricky dribbling display or behind-the-back pass had a purpose—to create easy baskets," said Most. "Cousy didn't try to embarrass the opponents; he wanted to outfox them. And he succeeded so often that Auerbach came to the conclusion that all he had to do was sit back and turn Cousy loose when it came to directing the Celtics' fastbreak attack."

Bob Cousy splits the Lakers defenders, James Paxon (left) and Bob Leonard (right), on his way to the basket. Hy Peskin/Time Life Pictures/Getty Images

Bill Russell (6) and Philadelphia's Wilt Chamberlin (13) battle during the 1965 Eastern Division championship series. Ken Regan/NBAE/Getty Images

"Havlicek Stole the Ball"
April 15, 1965

Throughout his career, Johnny Most always maintained a basic philosophy. "In my mind, I was always convinced the game I was about to broadcast would be the most important game I would ever announce," he said. "By looking at things that way, I was able to keep my enthusiasm at a high level every time I got behind the microphone." It was that attitude which made Johnny's crunch-time descriptions so exciting for his listeners over a 37-year span.

But one dramatic moment of announcing would stand above all others. It occurred at Boston Garden in the final seconds of the seventh game of the 1965 division championship against the Wilt Chamberlain-led Philadelphia 76ers. The home team had won each of the previous six games, giving the Celtics the clear advantage in the deciding matchup.

"Before the game, I sat in the press room with (color commentator) Jim Pansullo and (analyst) Al Grenert, who coached St. Anselm's. Both Al and I anticipated an easy Celtics victory. Jimmy predicted a Boston win, but only by a basket," Johnny recalled. "Boy, were Al and I wrong."

What made the game even more significant was that whichever team won would be the clear favorite to win the NBA title because the Lakers, who had already won the Western Division, were going into the finals without the services of 27-points-per-game scorer Elgin Baylor, who had suffered torn knee ligaments in LA's division title victory over Baltimore.

"I was really confident of a win," said Johnny. "Russell against Chamberlain in our building? For me, that was a Celtics advantage Philadelphia couldn't possibly overcome. At least that was my theory."

When Boston held an 18-point lead just eight minutes into the game, Johnny, by his own admission, became too cocky. "Wilt the Stilt Chamberlain is pouting. ...All his teammates are taking off-target jumpers from 25 feet away from the basket," Most elatedly yelled. "They're in a state of sheer panic."

The 76ers, however, regrouped and rallied to take a one-point lead at halftime. "That brought me back down to earth in a hurry," Most said. "For the rest of the game, I was a little nervous."

Even when Boston was up, 110-103, with a little more than a minute remaining, Johnny was discussing strategy with Grenert as Red started to light up his victory cigar. "Al suggested that Boston 'might want to foul Wilt (a 47-percent free throw shooter) every time he touches the ball,'" Johnny said. But the Celtics, with their seven-point lead, decided to play loose defense and make sure they didn't give up any three-point plays. The strategy almost backfired as Chamberlain scored six straight points, capped with an emphatic dunk.

Still, the Celtics had a one-point lead. Then the unimaginable happened. Russell in bounded the ball but his one-handed toss hit the guy wire holding the backboard.

"Russell lost the ball off the support," I bellowed into the microphone. "And the Celtics are claiming Chamberlain hit him on the arm. ...The ball goes over to Philadelphia. Time is out. And time is in for Jim Pansullo."

"Just five seconds left," Pansullo, an award-winning newsman, reminded the audience. But Philadelphia has the ball under the basket. Now this change of events, Al, has hit us right smack in the nose."

Grenert then predicted what the 76ers might do. "I think you'll see them get the ball into Chamberlain, or else you'll see (shooting guard Hal) Greer fool around with the ball for three or four seconds and then throw the thing at the basket. ...It's a real bad situation."

The team huddles broke and players jockeyed for position. Johnny Most, at his gravel-toned best, began his call, a moment that would establish him as an NBA legend:

John Havlicek steals the ball to preserve the Celtics' 110-109 victory over the 76ers.
Walter Iooss Jr./Sports Illustrated

"Greer is putting the ball into play. He gets it out deep. ...And Havlicek steals it...over to Sam Jones...Havlicek stole the ball. ...It's all over! It's all over!

"Johnny Havlicek is being mobbed by the fans. It's all over! ...A spectacular series comes to an end in spectacular fashion. Johnny Havlicek is being hoisted aloft. ...Bill Russell wants to grab him. He hugs him. He squeezes Havlicek.

"Havlicek saved this ballgame. Believe that! ...The Celtics win it, 110-109."

Most had no idea his description would become such a treasured memory for Celtics fans and for the league itself. "Immediately after the game, I thought my call had been a good one. With so little time to set the scene, the only fact I left out was that Greer's target was (76ers forward Chet) Walker," Johnny recalled. "Little did I imagine that my frantic, high-pitched call would become famous. I first began to realize that Boston fans enjoyed it when I heard it on TV and the radio almost every 15 minutes the next day. Fans would stop me on the street and ask me to 'do that Havlicek stole the ball thing.'"

Havlicek himself quickly became keenly aware of the call's enormous instant popularity. "Everywhere I go, people do their Johnny Most imitations (of the call)," the Celtics hero said to the broadcaster the day after the game. "Either I'm making you awfully famous or you're making me awfully famous. Which is it?"

Responded a kidding Johnny, "I think you deserve 99 percent of the glory. I'm satisfied with my little piece."

The one person who, to this day, doesn't enjoy hearing replays of Most's call is Dolph Schayes, who was the Philly coach that fateful day. "Every time I happen to see Havlicek—even now—I want to punch him in the nose," Schayes told Johnny decades later.

The 1984 NBA finals was billed as Larry Bird vs. Magic Johnson, but the actual series featured starring roles for their teammates. © Steve Lipofsky

The Henderson Steal
May 31, 1984

The hype surrounding the 1984 NBA finals between the Celtics and the Lakers revolved around one topic—the first postseason matchup of league MVP Larry Bird versus "Showtime Choreographer" Magic Johnson. The media had assigned supporting-role status to everyone else, well before the two teams actually stepped on the Boston Garden parquet court for the series' opening tipoff.

In Game 1, the player who dominated was the Lakers' 37-year-old Kareem Abdul-Jabbar, who scored 32 points as LA shocked the Celtics with a solid 115-109 victory.

Losing the first two games at home, according to Johnny Most, would have been a death wish for the Celtics. "This particular LA team has experience, depth, plenty of scorers, and a few guys who can be downright mean and dirty when they feel the urge," Johnny Most told partner Glenn Ordway prior to the game. "If the Celtics don't win this one, the Lakers will be like sharks smelling blood when the series gets back to LA. If there ever was a 'must-win' situation, this is it, babe."

And it certainly looked bleak for Boston in crunch time. After a three-point play on a James Worthy stuff put LA ahead, 113-111, the Celtics had an opportunity to tie when Kevin McHale was fouled with 20 seconds remaining. Uncharacteristically, the Boston power forward missed both free throws. Magic came down with the rebound on the second miss and the Lakers immediately called for a timeout.

As the teams talked strategy, Johnny and Glenn remarked that the timeout might turn out to be a break for Boston. "It was just a two-point game," Johnny recalled. "Glenn and I both were amazed the Lakers stopped the clock. We both commented that it was a mistake. I mean they had the ball in the hands of Magic, a great ball-handler and an 80-percent free throw shooter. That timeout gave us a slim chance to at least tie the game. It also gave the Celtics a chance to set their defense and go for a steal. If they didn't come up with one, there was still enough time left to foul and hope whoever went to the line would miss one or both of the free throws."

As LA's Byron Scott and Michael Cooper walked onto the court after the timeout, they congratulated each other. At that instant, Johnny had more than a hunch Boston could still produce a miracle. "There's still 18 seconds to play in this ball-game, and I've seen things happen that make guys have egg on their face when they have the early congratulations, the early celebrations. So, they have to play it out," he told the audience.

Gerald Henderson (43) played a key role in the 1984 championship. © Steve Lipofsky

Despite McHale hounding Worthy as he attempted to inbound the ball, the Laker forward managed to get the ball in to Magic, who immediately shoveled a pass back to an open Worthy. Danny Ainge, the closest Celtic, was a full ten feet away. Instead of holding the ball and waiting to be fouled, Worthy quickly threw a long, soft lob pass in the direction of Scott.

And that's precisely the split second when Johnny's voice crackled: "...And it's picked off. ...Goes to Henderson. ...He lays it up and in. ...It's all tied up. ... A great play by Henderson. ...They threw a cross-court pass. ...And Henderson anticipated it and picked it off."

Johnny later would say, "The call went from a conversational tone to my Saniflush shout."

Reflecting on the Henderson steal call, Johnny said, "I was almost as excited as when Havlicek stole the ball. But there were differences. Havlicek's steal preserved a win; Henderson's prevented a potentially devastating loss. The Havlicek play ended a game and a series; Gerald's play didn't settle the outcome. It did, in all probability, change the outcome."

To this day, Henderson claims he has never heard Johnny's call of his steal. "I have this image in my mind of Johnny going wild, with a cigarette in his mouth, straining his voice and barking out, 'Henderson stole the ball.' That's how I want to remember things."

Cedric Maxwell and Red Auerbach celebrate the 1984 NBA championship after a dramatic seven-game series. © Steve Lipofsky

A smug Isiah Thomas (11) thought a Game 5 win was in the bag with only five seconds remaining, but Larry Bird (33) had one more trick up his sleeve. © Steve Lipofsky

The Bird Steal
May 26, 1987

It was clearly one of the most desperate moments in Celtics franchise history. The Eastern Conference finals against Detroit was tied 2-2, but KC Jones's troops were literally on their last legs as they attempted a fourth-quarter comeback against the Pistons at the Garden in Game 5. Boston was hurting at both power forward and center. Kevin McHale's fractured navicular bone left him with a pronounced limp, Robert Parish was moving at three-quarters speed due to a sprained ankle, and Bill Walton was dressed but hardly able to even jog because of a broken bone in his foot.

Only five seconds remained on the clock after Larry Bird's runner from the left side was blocked by Dennis Rodman and bounced out of bounds, last touched by Jerry Sichting. Holding a 107-106 lead, the cocky and physical "Bad Boys" had the upset just about wrapped up.

Or so thought Pistons floor leader Isiah Thomas.

Detroit coach Chuck Daly was frantically yelling and signaling for a timeout, but Thomas either didn't get the message or simply decided to ignore it. Had he called for time, Detroit could have set up its play past halfcourt. Instead Thomas quickly tried to inbound the ball as Sichting pressured him. Isiah spotted what appeared to be an open man, Bill Laimbeer, standing eight feet from the baseline. Fortunately for the Celtics, Bird, standing near the foul line, noticed the uncovered Laimbeer a split second before Thomas did.

At that instant, Johnny Most double-clutched his vocal chords into high gear: "And...there's a steal by Bird...underneath to DJ. ...He lays it in...right at one second left."

Johnny, who occasionally referred to himself as a "rock and roll sportscaster," had another hit call on his hands. It would be replayed repeatedly on both local and national TV. "It wasn't perfect," he said afterwards. "You can't rehearse a bang-bang play like that. And you can never, never anticipate what Larry Bird might do out there. How can you? I've seen him do the impossible too many times.

"This steal was just an incredible all-around display of court sense. First of all, Bird ran in and snatched the ball with one hand. Then he somehow managed to tiptoe along the baseline, staying inbounds. On top of everything else, he throws a perfect pass to a cutting Dennis Johnson for the game-winning basket. And he did it all in three seconds."

Following Larry Bird's dramatic steal, the Celtics put the clamps on Detroit and capped the 108-107 win. All photos © Steve Lipofsky

55

"The Mad Bomber," Danny Ainge, participates in the 1987 Three-Point Shoot Out.

Calling the Shots:
The Big Three-Pointers

rom the moment Celtics guard Chris Ford nailed the NBA's first three-point bomb on Columbus Day of 1979, the day Larry Bird made his pro debut, Johnny Most knew the long-distance shot would add excitement to his broadcasts.

"The old ABA, which folded in 1976, brought the three-point shot into basketball. Like the red, white and blue basketballs the league used, the three-pointer was more a gimmick to draw fans than anything else. The ABA game was designed to showcase offense. It was a fast-paced, up-tempo style of play. Nobody paid much attention to defense," Most said. "The more points you put up, the better. Make things as flashy as possible; that was the ABA's philosophy.

"When the NBA adopted the three-pointer, the shot really became more of a tactical weapon. Boston, as much, if not more, than any other team, was able to use the shot to its advantage in the early to mid-'80s. Why? First of all, you had Bird, the greatest clutch outside shooter in the game. You also had (Danny) Ainge, the mad bomber, who would shoot a three on a two-on-one fastbreak. He had that much confidence in his long-range jumper. The Celtics also had Ford, (M.L.) Carr, Henderson, then DJ and (Scott) Wedman—all good shooters from behind the line. Even (Kevin) McHale eventually would take the shot if the defense backed off him.

"The key to Boston's three-point success, in my mind, was its strength inside, combined with excellent ball movement. (Cedric) Maxwell, Bird, (Robert) McHale and Walton were all guys who could do a lot of damage down low. Opponents had no choice but to double-team those guys. When that happened, they would pass the ball around until someone got open outside the three-point line. The shot became an absolutely devastating weapon."

Which made for some great broadcasting moments high above courtside because, the Celtics, especially Bird, didn't hesitate to use the three-pointer in crucial situations. "Oh, boy, do I love that shot," Johnny said. "It can be a halfcourt heave, a desperation shot as the 24-second clock winds down, or it can decide a game's outcome. Doesn't matter. There's that feeling of pure elation when a three-pointer goes through the basket."

Larry Bird helped Boston win some big games during his career, including three NBA championships. Jonathan Kirn/NBAE/Getty Images

The Game Winner

Johnny Most remembered the night Larry Bird torched the Suns at the old Coliseum.

"There were four or five seconds remaining. Boston was down by two. After a Celtics timeout, Bird, totally unfazed by the situation, was standing right in front of me on the sidelines," Johnny said. "As the teams set up for the inbounds play, Larry began to talk to Phoenix forward Alvin Scott, the man who would be guarding him. 'You'd better be covering me good because I'm taking a three-pointer to win this thing,' Bird said. I started laughing, and so did Scott. Then Bird inbounded the ball, got it back, and swished a three at the buzzer. As Scott started to walk off the court, Larry yelled at him, 'Damn it, Alvin, I told you what I was going to do. Why didn't you listen to me?' That's really who Larry Bird is. He doesn't know the meaning of the word 'pressure.' I mean he's having fun out there when everyone else, including myself, is nervous."

No one was better than Johnny at describing the tenseness and the excitement of a possible game-deciding play. "It's safe to say you can hear it in my voice," Most said. "I get just as emotional as the fans who are listening to the game. Like them, I'm hoping for the best, but I'm not expecting the Celtics to win. I'm on pins and needles—and I want my listeners to know it. Then I see Bird with the ball. People say my voice changes. They say I start to sound like sandpaper scraping a rough surface. I'm just waiting for something unbelievable to happen. With Larry, you anticipate. You sense something great will happen; you just don't know exactly what."

Johnny Most looked like the big man on campus when he filled in as Boston College's football play-by-play announcer in 1976. Photo courtesy of the Most family

Johnny and Gino
Call BC Football
October 9, 1976

*I*t may come as a surprise to almost every Boston College football fan, but Johnny Most once filled in as the Eagles' play-by-play man, teaming up with Patriots legend Gino Cappeletti for a 1976 clash against 13th-ranked Florida State.

"The game was at Alumni Stadium," recalled then-BC sports information director Reid Oslin. "Our play-by-play man, Gil Santos, was out of town covering the Patriots, so WBZ Radio asked Johnny if he might be able to work the broadcast. He jumped at the opportunity to handle football for the first time since he had been Marty Glickman's partner for the New York Football Giants in 1955."

The Eagles, coached by Joe Yukica and captained by linebacker Peter Cronan, had won their opening three games, including a one-point victory over highly favored Texas. On the other hand, the Seminoles were rebuilding their program under first-year head coach Bobby Bowden.

"This was a huge game for us," said Oslin, who today heads BC's public affairs staff. "Johnny knew our team well and obviously had done some research on Florida State. He sounded great, like the old pro that he was. Unfortunately, Florida State played a great game and beat us, 28-9."

Cappeletti said the broadcast went smoothly. "To be honest, I don't remember any details of the broadcast, other than that Johnny and I had a great time working together," Gino said recently. "We were old pals. He and Tommy Heinsohn used to come into my nightclub, The Point After, following Celtics games. We'd talk sports until closing time, sometimes later. Those two were quite the characters."

(From left) Larry Bird, Dr. J, Moses Malone and Robert Parish exchange words before punches started flying. © Steve Lipofsky

Bird Gets Ambushed
By Dr. J & Co.
November 9, 1984

An avid boxing fan, Johnny Most saw nothing wrong with a good, clean fight on the court. "Basketball is—and always has been—a contact sport. Don't let anyone tell you otherwise. When you have guys that tall and that wide pushing and shoving for rebounds, there are going to be skirmishes every now and then," he said. "Boston has had its share of tough guys. Bob Brannum, Jim Loscutoff, Wayne Embry, David Cowens, none of them would ever back down from anyone. I mean these guys really enjoyed it when some guy would be foolish enough to challenge them to a fight. And Red Auerbach wanted players with that type of toughness on his team. He'd say that every great team needs at least one guy who can intimidate the opponents, who is always willing to exchange a few punches in order to protect his teammates. I agree with him completely."

But when Julius Erving and Larry Bird, the league's MVP in '83-'84, squared off with less than two minutes remaining in the fourth quarter of a Celtics-Sixers matchup at the Garden, things heated up. "Philadelphia was getting crushed, and Larry had flat out embarrassed Dr. J, outscoring him 42-6. He was, I'm sure, giving Julius the business in a comical sort of way," Johnny said. "Erving didn't see the humor in Bird's remarks. ...Both threw elbows. ...They both seemed to become unglued and started exchanging punches while grabbing each other's throats. Those type of things happen in games involving such intense rivals. What happened after that was positively inexcusable."

After Philly coach Billy Cunningham stepped onto the court towards Bird near the 76ers bench, Moses Malone came up from behind the Celtics forward. As Malone and Charles Barkley held Bird's arms, Erving landed several more punches to Bird's face.

Johnny became irate: "Malone blindsides Bird. ...Malone tackled Bird and put him in a headlock. ...Now Bird wants Julius. ...A real yellow, cowardly act. ...Malone is a coward. I mean I'll say that irrevocably. He's a coward. ...They don't like being humiliated like this, but this fight humiliates them further because they were cowards in this fight."

Houston's Ralph Sampson fields questions from the media after his run-in with the Celtics. Andrew D. Bernstein/NBAE/Getty Images

Big Ralph Sampson's
"Gutless Streak"
June 5, 1986

The Celtics were in the process of dissecting the Rockets and winning their 16th NBA championship. Up 3-1 in the '86 finals, Boston was attempting to add the finishing touches to what had been a relatively easy series against Houston and its Twin Towers, 7'0" Akeem Olajuwon and 7'4" Ralph Sampson.

Early in the second quarter of Game 5 at the Summit, 6-1 Boston guard Jerry Sichting found himself guarding Sampson after Houston, in transition, forced the Celtics to scramble on defense. About all Sichting could do to prevent an easy basket was to push the Rockets' big man in the back.

Frustrated with Boston's point guard's scrappy defense, Sampson threw an elbow that hit its intended target, Sichting's head. Johnny and partner Glenn Ordway were outraged as fireworks erupted.

"And now they're fighting. ...Sampson started the WHOLE DAMN THING. ...Big Ralph Sampson, the big brave bull, picking on a guy 6'1", a foot and three inches smaller than he is. ..." Johnny emphatically explained.

As the fight escalated, Bill Walton grabbed Sampson near the sideline, and Dennis Johnson took a punch to the face. "Now it's getting into the crowd. Now it's getting dangerous. Now here's where it could really get nasty," screamed Ordway. "The police now are coming out on the court. ...Sampson now kicks the ball."

Johnny was still on a tirade: "Sampson is the last guy who has a right to complain. ...He started it. He threw the first punch He hit Sichting and he hit him hard. And Sichting objected to it. ...And Sampson said, 'I'm Ralph Sampson. I have a right to hit you. I have a right to BREAK YOUR HEAD.'...Well, Ralph Sampson showed his true colors. HE IS A GUTLESS BIG GUY WHO PICKS ON THE LITTLE PEOPLE. ...I'll tell you, he really showed me a gutless streak."

Bill Laimbeer pleads with the referees. © Steve Lipofsky

The "Yellow" Bad Boys
Tackle Bird
May 23, 1987

ollowing Johnny's description of the Pistons' mugging of Larry Bird in Game 3 of the '87 playoffs, every Detroit player refused to be interviewed by either Most or his color commentator, Glenn Ordway.

"They were being crybabies," said Most. "It was typical childishness, orchestrated by Little Lord Fauntleroy himself, Isiah Thomas. All I did was accurately portray how the Pistons were a dirty, filthy team."

It all started innocently enough as Johnny, in subdued tones, was simply following a Celtics' set play. As Bird attempted an off-balance layup, Bill Laimbeer fouled the three-time NBA MVP by putting him in a headlock and bulldogging him to the floor.

Johnny was more than mildly upset.

"There's a violent, violent knockdown by Laimbeer, and Bird just smacked him. ...Oh, my...a completely unnecessary foul by Laimbeer, and Laimbeer got walloped. ...Now Rodman wants him. Now Bird is throwing Rodman away. ...OH, THE YEL-LOW, GUTLESS WAY THEY DO THINGS HERE. ...Now Isiah Thomas is coming over. ...They have been called a dirty ballclub AND I CAN SEE WHY. ...This is a typical disgusting display by Rodman, Laimbeer and Thomas. AND THEY TOLD ME I SHOULDN'T SAY BAD THINGS ABOUT ISIAH—AND I SAY 'WHY NOT?'"

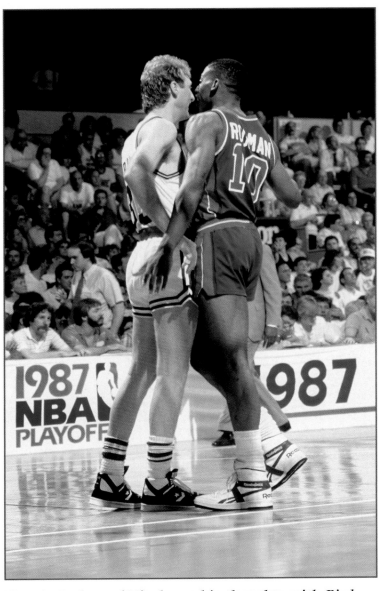

Dennis Rodman (10) shares his thoughts with Bird
about his retaliation for the hard Laimbeer foul.
© Steve Lipofsky

In Johnny Most's oft-vocalized opinion, Bill Laimbeer should have won an Oscar for best actor. © Steve Lipofsky

Garfield Heard is heavily pressured by Boston's defense during overtime.
AP/WWP

The 3OT Win Over Phoenix
June 4, 1976

When John Havlicek hit a running bank shot as time was running out in Game 5's second overtime of the Celtics-Suns '76 Finals, Boston appeared to have secured a comfortable 3-2 series advantage.

At first, Johnny thought so, as did the Garden crowd, which poured out onto the parquet floor to celebrate. His joyous call of Jarrin' John's clutch basket: "The pass goes to Havlicek. He's coming around from the left. The shot is good, the ballgame's over. It's all over. The shot is good. ..."

Minutes later, Most gave his audience some bad news: "They (the officials) say there's one second left."

Still, Boston held a 111-110 lead, with a mere tick remaining on the game clock. After the Celtics had been summoned back to the court from their locker room, play was set to resume.

The Suns had no timeouts left, but Phoenix guard Paul Westphal called for one any-how. It was, as Boston center Dave Cowens, said, "a heads-up move." Although the Suns received a technical for the extra timeout, under the rules at that time, Phoenix was allowed to advance the ball to halfcourt. Celtics guard JoJo White converted the 'T', putting Phoenix down by two.

The ensuing inbounds play was a pass from Suns forward Curtis Perry to teammate Garfield Heard, who was 18 feet away from the basket. With Boston forward Don Nelson playing "in-his-shirt" defense, all Heard had time to do was take a turn-around. Swish. Heard had beat the buzzer and forced a third OT. "I am sitting here in absolute disbelief at the way this thing has gone," said a stunned and obviously disappointed Most.

Johnny's emotionalism returned late in overtime number 3. "JoJo drives, lays it off to McDonald. ...And McDonald puts them ahead, 120-118, 1:35 left in the overtime." After Heard missed a jumper, Havlicek found McDonald along the baseline and Most's voice began to crack, "The fallaway is good...Glenn McDonald, Glen McDonald."

Although Phoenix would again close to within two in the final seconds, this game was destined to earn McDonald a place in NBA and Celtics history. His defensive rebound and two free throws clinched the win for Boston.

High above courtside, Most was rooting hard for another in a long line of Boston role players/heroes. "I'll tell ya, for a kid who had lost his confidence, he's just scored six straight clutch points," said the gleeful Celtics announcer. "And I'll bet you he's just got his confidence back."

Coach Bill Fitch smiles as he heads to the locker room to celebrate the 1981 Eastern Conference championship. AP/WWP

The 1981 Eastern Conference Finals vs. Philly

After a heartbreaking 107-105 loss to the 76ers at the Spectrum, the Celtics were behind, 3-1, in the '81 Eastern Conference finals. In his postgame talk to the Boston players, general manager Red Auerbach took a positive approach.

"I told them that Philadelphia still had to win one more game," Auerbach said. "This series won't be over if we can stop them from winning one game. That's all we have to do."

Red's positive spin to Boston's deficit might have been a factor when the Celtics returned to the Garden for Game 5. Trailing 109-103 with less than two minutes left in regulation, the Celtics scored eight straight, capped by guard M.L. Carr's two free throws. Center Robert Parish then preserved the win with a perfectly timed steal of a Philly pass.

Boston remained optimistic, but the 76ers were heading home where they had beaten the Celtics 11 straight times dating back to 1979. Midway through the second quarter, Philly looked to be in cruise control, holding a 17-point lead. The Celtics gradually fought back with inspired play at both ends of the court, including sixth man Kevin McHale's block of a possible game-tying shot by "The Boston Strangler," Andrew Toney, which sent Johnny into orbit: "Back now to Toney. ...Toney looks, drops his head...he's going...AND IT'S BLOCKED BY (vocal chords straining) Mc---H-A-L-E. ...And the Celtics have kept this series alive. They have won here tonight for the first time since 1979."

Both teams knew Game 7 at the Garden would be a dogfight. It was Philly which seemed to be in command, leading 89-82 with five minutes left. The Celtics brought the Sixers' offense to a dead stop. Philadelphia was held without a field goal for the remainder of the game. With 1:10 left and the score tied, the Celtics defense stiffened, creating another dramatic moment for Johnny: "Erving pumps a little bit, goes on the pick and roll, the ball is loose, (Philly center Daryl) Dawkins has it now, tries to force it up and it's no good. ...And Bird's got the rebound. Bird is coming up the left. The stop and pop off the glass IS GOOD. Boston leads, 91-89."

Sixers point guard Mo Cheeks had a chance to tie the score at the foul line in the waning seconds, but he could make only one of two free throws. Just before the buzzer, sounded, Philadelphia had one more slim chance.

"And the pass hits the top of the backboard and. ...IT'S OVER. IT'S OVER. It was an alley-oop pass," Johnny shouted. "...They have come from three-to-one down and they have won the series. It's over. IT'S ALL OVER."

Magic Johnson (32) looks to pass upcourt during Game 2 of the 1984 Finals.
AP/WWP

The 1984
Title Series vs. the Lakers

As previously mentioned, Gerald Henderson's famed steal in Game 2 of Boston's '84 showdown with the Lakers gave the Celtics a fighting chance to even the series, tying the score, 113-113. However, LA still had 13 seconds to produce a "Magic Moment" in regulation at the Boston Garden.

After successfully inbounding the ball from halfcourt, the Lakers put the ball in Johnson's hands. Johnny went to work again: "It goes quickly over to (Lakers guard Byron) Scott. Scott holds the ball, over to Magic. Down to nine seconds...Magic holding the ball. Magic trying to work on (Cedric) Maxwell. Magic has still got it. Down to two seconds. One second. He's going to have to shoot it. HE DOESN'T GET IT OFF. They get no shot at all. THEY HAD THIRTEEN SECONDS AND THEY DID NOT GET A SHOT OFF."

In overtime, a Scott Wedman jumper from 18 feet on the left side gave Boston a 123-121 lead with 14 seconds to go. Then Robert Parish sealed the Celtics' classic comeback win by stealing the ball from Laker veteran Bob McAdoo.

When LA crushed Boston, 137-104, at the Forum in Game 3, the "so-called experts," as Most referred to anyone and everyone who didn't unconditionally back the Celtics, were confident LA would end the series quickly.

Bird himself was ultra-critical of his team following the worst defeat in franchise playoff history. "We played like a bunch of sissies," he told the media. "We've got some great players on this team, but we don't have the players sometimes with the heart that we need." Meanwhile, the Lakers were loose, talking about "entertaining the fans" and "moving and grooving" with their "Showtime" fastbreak offense.

At halftime of Game 4, the Lakers were still on a roll against the almost defenseless Celtics, holding a ten-point advantage. However, Bird sent a message to the Lakers when he literally rear-ended inbounds defender Michael Cooper up and over photographers' row early in the third quarter. "Cooper's looking around, wondering what truck just hit him," Most joked. "That's what the Celtics have to do. They have to get tough and play more physically. Punish the Lakers for their sheer arrogance."

Kevin McHale, known for his finesse game, followed Bird's example when he clotheslined Laker power forward Kurt Rambis on an LA fastbreak layup attempt. Johnny loved what he was seeing. "Rambis is decked. OH, YOU DON'T DARE TOUCH HIM! You don't dare. He was really decked by McHale and he didn't like it

Larry Bird puts heavy pressure on Lakers forward Kurt Rambis in Game 1 of the Finals. AP/WWP

at all. HE GOES AROUND BELTING PEOPLE ALL THROUGH THE BALL-GAME, BUT WHEN HE GETS HIT, HE CANNOT TAKE IT."

Minutes later, Bird would go nose to nose with Kareem Abdul-Jabbar after the Lakers center tossed an elbow that landed squarely on Bird's jaw. Kareem had lost his cool. "Larry was right in Abdul-Jabbar's shirt. Kareem was trying to back Bird down and Bird wouldn't give an inch. ...That's when Jabbar started throwing elbows."

With :04 left in regulation, the game was tied 113-113. The Celtics got the ball to Bird, whose long-distance runner caromed off the basket and into McHale's hands. The Celtic forward's rebound jumper from five feet away beat the buzzer but bounced off the rim.

In overtime, two missed free throws by Magic, who was in the midst of what Johnny would later call a series-long "personal nightmare," gave Boston a chance to take the lead with less than a half-minute to go. The Celtics obviously would be looking for Bird. Johnny painted the

Robert Parish (left) and Dennis Johnson (3) force Kareem Abdul-Jabbar to pass in Game 7. AP/WWP

picture: "Maxwell looking...Bird rotates in. Bird pops out. Avoids a steal. Gets it over to DJ. Bird goes right into the pivot. ...Back into Bird. The fallaway IS GOOD. ...And it was Magic who was defending."

Down by two, the Lakers had an opportunity to tie when James Worthy was fouled, but he missed his first free throw. As the ball hit the court, Maxwell casually walked across the lane, smiled, turned, and gave the "choke sign" to Worthy. The second foul shot was good, cutting the Celtics' lead to 125-124. Now LA had no choice but to foul with only 12 seconds remaining. When DJ converted two free throws, the Lakers called timeout to set up for a three-point shot that could tie the game. Worthy, looking for Magic, inbounded the ball, but M.L. Carr sniffed out the play, stole the ball, and went in for a stuff to seal the Boston victory, evening the finals at 2-2.

Back in Boston, with temperatures surpassing 90 degrees in the Garden, Bird's 34-point, 17-rebound effort led the Celtics to a 121-103 win and a 3-2 series edge. The teams then traveled cross-country to LA, where the Lakers outscored Boston by 22 points over the final 16 minutes to win going away, 119-108, and evening the series, 3-3. The deciding game, however, would be played on the parquet floor.

At the end of three, the Celtics had a 13-point lead. "The Lakers are running on an empty tank," Most said, as the teams waited for play to resume. "Kareem's got his face buried in a wet towel...(LA coach Pat) Riley's hair is so sweaty that all that grease he uses on it is dripping on his $1,000 suit. ...Magic is just sitting there silently."

Two baskets by DJ kept Boston in front down the stretch. Then the Celtics put on a defensive clinic. "All right, Cooper goes to the left. Now back over to Magic. Magic wants to go. ...AND IT'S STOLEN AWAY BY DJ," Johnny barked. Two possessions later, the Lakers attempted to make one final run. "Magic goes behind his back. ...He tries to get the shot off. ...IT'S STOLEN AWAY BY DJ. It was blocked by Kevin...DJ to the basket...and he's fouled."

The Celtics' 15th championship celebration was underway. "Now Carr and Maxwell do a Magic Johnson imitation. ...There they go again. They do the high-five in the air and then point at each other," said Johnny, between deep inhales of his cigarette.

General manager Red Auerbach, trademark cigar in mouth, celebrates the 1984 NBA championship. AP/WWP

Kevin McHale hits a jumper during his 56-point effort against the Detroit Pistons.
© Steve Lipofsky

McHale's 56-Point Record
March 3, 1985

Kevin McHale was on a game-long roll as the Garden crowd cheered him on. Twenty-one of his first 28 shots had fallen against Detroit as Piston defenders Bill Laimbeer, Earl Cureton, Kent Benson and Major Jones took turns in "the torture chamber," trying to guard the Celtics power forward in the paint. With two minutes remaining, McHale's point total stood at 52, a basket short of the Celtics' all-time individual scoring record set by John Havlicek in an April 1, 1973 playoff game against Atlanta.

Johnny Most was all pumped up: "Bird very quickly gets the ball down to McHale. AND McHALE HITS IT. McHALE BREAKS THE (regular-season) RECORD. ...McHale has 54 points, which ties Havlicek for the all-time Celtics scoring record in one game. All right, he gets the pass from Bird...triple-teamed. ...Back over to Bird, back into McHale. AND HE GETS FOULED. ...And the shot is good. That breaks the record. ...The (second) shot is good. McHale has 56."

Larry Bird shoots over his Atlanta rival, Dominique Wilkins.
Scott Cunningham/NBAE/Getty Images

Bird Rips Through
Atlanta for 60
March 12, 1985

Nine days after Kevin McHale's 56-point, 22-for-29 record effort left Johnny searching for superlatives to describe the Celtics power forward's skills, Larry Bird came up with another one-game highlight film for the ages.

Playing against the Hawks in New Orleans, the "Hick from French Lick" was in a zone. Johnny couldn't believe his own eyes as Bird nailed one shot after another: "I mean he absolutely cannot miss no matter how closely they're guarding him."

(Exactly one month earlier, Bird had destroyed the Jazz at the Salt Palace by recording a triple-double in just the first three quarters, as well as coming up with nine steals. Instead of going for the rare quadruple-double, Bird opted to take a seat on the bench. "I've never played for stats," he said. "I play for wins." At one point in that game, Bird jokingly asked Utah coach Frank Layden, "Don't you have anybody who can guard me, Frank?" Layden turned, took a long look down his bench, walked back toward Bird, and then answered with a quick "Nope.")

Despite Bird's unmerciful offensive attack, the Hawks, behind Dominique Wilkins, had managed to "hang around" as the game entered the final three minutes. So, Larry Joe kept on firing. Johnny quickened his pace with each field goal attempt: "All right, McHale gets the ball over to Bird. Bird steps around his man. Goes in for a high runner. It's good. ...On the right, Bird on a popout. SWISH, from the corner. ...DJ gets it in the corner to Bird...Bird upfakes. Bird takes the shot. HE'S GOT IT. He's got 54. ...DJ wants to get it to Bird. He gets it to Bird. And Bird takes the shot. HE'S GOT IT FROM THE SIDELINE. AND THEY TOOK IT AWAY FROM HIM. (Referee) Hubie Evans says it's no basket. He called a foul. He's got to go to the line. ...All right, DJ has it. Back to Bird. Driving into the lane. HE'S GOT IT. HE'S GOT IT. HE'S GOT 60 POINTS. LARRY BIRD HAS JUST SCORED 60 POINTS."

Some of Bird's greatest games were played against Dominique Wilkins and the Atlanta Hawks. © Steve Lipofsky

Bird vs. Wilkins
May 22, 1988

*I*ndividual playoff matchups seldom live up to their advance billing. Perhaps, though, the most notable exception took place throughout Game 7 of the '88 Eastern Conference semifinals when Larry Bird and Dominique Wilkins "just went at each other," as Most termed it.

While Wilkins guarded Bird on defense, it was principally Kevin McHale who was given the assignment to cover the Hawks star. At the end of three quarters, Wilkins was winning the shootout, 31-14, but the Celtics led 84-82. And Bird was just warming up.

As Johnny continued his play-by-play, he would dryly mention a Wilkins basket and then "go through the roof" when Bird would answer. "And (Atlanta guard John) Battle has a notion. Goes for a drive. Gets swallowed up. Back to Dominique for three. And he has a three," Most said stoically. At the other end of the court, though, Bird's shooting got Johnny's juices flowing again: "Five seconds left (on the shot clock). It goes to Bird. Four seconds. Bird drives. Lays it up. IT IS GOOD. IT'S GOOD. A STUMBLING, FALLING SHOT. (Atlanta coach) MIKE FRATELLO WAS SCREAMING 'TRAVELING.' SURE, HE TRAVELED—BECAUSE YOUR GUY RIPPED HIM. THERE'S A FOUL ON THE PLAY. THE BASKET WILL COUNT."

With 47 seconds left and Boston up by a basket, Johnny's emotions went to extremes once again: "(Atlanta forward Antoine) Carr on the cut to Dominique. HE GOT REJECTED. And they're going to call a foul. 'The Untouchable' goes to the line. And he hits." On the next play, Most bounced right back from the momentary Celtics setback: "DJ coming up. DJ sets it up on the right side. Now he wants Bird. Gets it into Bird…Bird gets mauled. And they don't call it. But he goes in from right to left WITH A RIGHT-HANDED SCOOP SHOT."

Johnny would leave the broadcasting booth with a smile on his face as Bird's 20 fourth-quarter points (only one missed field goal) lifted the Celtics to a 118-116 victory and a trip to the Eastern Conference Finals.

Johnny Being Johnny

It seems everyone has a favorite Johnny Most story. He was a legendary broadcaster and an NBA pioneer. It's an indisputable fact that he was also one of the game's most colorful characters.

One of his early classics on the air came in 1959 during a game at the Garden against Syracuse. Boston had an 18-point lead early in the third quarter of Game 5 at the Garden. "When Russell made an unbelievable block, I began to shout, 'Russell came from out of nowhere. ...' Just then, my false teeth popped out of my mouth and headed over the balcony railing. In desperation, I reached out with my right hand and snatched my choppers just before they started heading downward towards the people in the loge seats. I quickly put them back in. After sheepishly explaining to my audience what had just occurred, I turned to my color commentator, longtime and highly respected St. Anselm coach Al Grenert, and proudly stated, 'How's that for quick hands?'"

- Massachusetts state representative Brian Wallace still talks about his first day on the job as a Celtics ballboy in 1954:

  "I wanted to meet Johnny just as much as I wanted to meet the players. Just before Most headed for his broadcast booth, I approached him and asked if there was anything I could get him. 'Thanks, kid,' Johnny said. 'Do me a favor, will ya? Get me four cokes, two coffees with extra cream, and two packs of English Ovals.' By the time the game ended, all he had left were a few cigarettes."

- Former Celtic Togo Palazzi cannot forget the day he debuted as Babson's head coach:

  "Johnny showed up for the game to support me. Instead of watching from the stands, he walked straight to the bench, sitting down near me. I was surprised but didn't say anything. Five minutes into the game, the refs made a call against us. Johnny jumped off the bench and started arguing with the officials. That cost my team a technical. Three minutes later, there was another questionable call. This time Johnny storms out on the court and starts berating the officials. He got a second 'T' and had to be escorted from the gym by the campus police. I can't say I wasn't relieved to see him go."

Celtics GM Red Auerbach hugs stars Bill Russell (left) and John Havlicek (right) after they led Boston to the 1968 title. AP/WWP

- Tommy Heinsohn remembers when he first entered sportscasting, handling Boston's television play-by-play:

    "I asked Johnny for some tips. We sat down for at least a couple hours and he gave me some excellent advice. At the end of the conversation, I told Johnny that I still felt nervous about my new job. He replied, 'Just relax. You'll do fine.' Then Johnny paused and added one last remark, 'Besides, nobody watching on TV will hear you anyway. They'll all be listening to me.'"

- Of course, there was the time Johnny startled Rick Barry by asking the cocky Warriors star, "Tell me, Rick, when did you first start falling in love with yourself?"

- How about "Free Bagel Night" in Milwaukee? That was the game in which Johnny interrupted his play-by-play and angrily exclaimed, "The audacity of these fans. I've just got hit with another piece of bagel. What a bunch of morons these people are!"

Johnny Most and partner Glenn Ordway (right) prepare for another thrilling Celtics broadcast. © Steve Lipofsky

- Longtime fans of Most's broadcasts still recall his description of a David Cowens's foul: "Ladies and gentlemen, you're not going to believe this but Kareem Abdul-Jabbar has just stuck his eye on Cowens's elbow."

- Veteran broadcaster Jim Karvellas remembers the night in Detroit when Johnny was battling a severe case of laryngitis:

  "I was handling the Celtics-Pistons game for USA Network on cable in the mid-'70s. An hour before tipoff, I saw Johnny in the pressroom before the game. He couldn't talk. I mean he was really struggling with his voice—and he was doing that particular game by himself. I told Johnny I'd try to find someone who could fill in for him, but Johnny just waved me off.

  "Then he took out a jar of Vicks Vapo-Rub. I didn't think rubbing Vicks on his neck would do much good at all. Next thing I knew, Johnny stuck his fingers in the jar, grabbed a gob of Vicks and stuck it down his throat to coat it. It looked gross, but, to my amazement, it made Johnny feel better. His voice was still almost shot, but he managed to get through the entire broadcast."

- For ex-Celtic Rick Weitzman, who was Johnny's partner in the late '70s and early '80s, Johnny's war of words with Bullets center-power forward Jeff Ruland's (McFilthy's) mom tops the list of memories:

  "We were doing a game at Washington and I approached Ruland before the opening game and asked him if he would do a five-minute pregame interview.

  "'You work with that Most guy, don't you?' Ruland said. 'Well, my mother listens to your broadcasts from Long Island and she says you guys are (expletive deleted). She tells me Most's play-by-play is nothing but happy horse crap. Forget about me doing any interview for you stiffs.'

  "I went back to Johnny and told him about my conversation with Ruland. When he went on the air, he gave his standard introduction. Then, without pausing, he added, 'By the way, Mrs. Ruland, if you're listening to this broadcast back in New York, you'd better turn off the radio because you're not going to like what you hear.'"

- Larry Bird certainly enjoyed the constant pranks Danny Ainge would play on Johnny:

  "I guess the best was when Danny got ahold of Johnny's cigarettes and put loads (tiny, harmless explosive sticks) in every single butt. Every time Johnny would light one up, the tip of the cigarette would explode. The funniest thing was that Johnny would just throw it away and light up another. If we didn't stop him, every single cigarette in the pack would have exploded on him. That's how much he loved to smoke.

"Every time Ainge tricked him, Johnny would pretend to be mad. He'd call Danny a 'young Mormon punk' or a 'brat.' But you knew it was an act. Johnny enjoyed a good joke, even at his own expense."

- Cowens's favorite "Most Moment" occurred at a birthday party thrown for Johnny:

"This took place when Johnny first was required to breathe into his nose through a small tube connected to an oxygen tank. There were quite a few people at the party but they all seemed to be ignoring Johnny, who was sitting alone in one corner of this huge room. My first reaction was to wonder why all his friends and family were being rude.

"I immediately decided I'd cheer him up and keep him company for awhile. As I pulled up a chair and sat down next to him, I glanced down at his hand and realized that he was holding a lit cigarette—about an inch away from the oxygen tank. It took me about a mini-second to sprint across the room and join all the other guests. Once I made it to 'relative safety,' I looked over at Johnny, who stared back at me with that impish grin of his. I could read his mind. It was like he was thinking, 'Boy, did I just scare the crap out of you.'"

- Johnny's broadcast partner for much of the '80s, Glenn Ordway, has many tales:

"I guess the best was when Johnny set his pants on fire at the Garden. It happened just as the game ended. There were four huge holes near the crotch as Johnny used some of his coffee to douse the fire. I had to give a summary and do a commercial, but I was laughing so much that the words just wouldn't come out."

- Glenn also has vivid memories of the night Boston was playing the Warriors on the road during the '87-'88 season:

"Johnny was supposed to interview KC Jones for the pregame show. However, no one could find Johnny. I filled in while our producer, Tom Carelli, hunted for him. Just before tipoff, Tom found Johnny chatting with his old roommate and close friend, (ex-Celtic) Don Barksdale, in an unused locker room.

"'Johnny,' Tom said to him, 'you're going to miss the show.'

"'Remember one thing, kid,' Johnny shouted at Carelli. 'I AM the (expletive deleted) show. Got it?'

Glenn Ordway (left) and Johnny Most get in the Christmas spirit. © Steve Lipofsky

(From left) Robert Parish, Larry Bird and Kevin McHale all have their share of favorite Most moments. AP/WWP

"Carelli came running back to me and relayed Johnny's comments. Larry Bird happened to be close by and overheard what Johnny had said.

"Larry then went out on the court and scored 41 points as Boston beat Golden State 115-110. When Bird stepped onto the bus, he tapped Johnny on the shoulder and kidded him, 'Remember one thing, Johnny. I'M the (expletive deleted) show. Got it?' Johnny nodded his head in agreement as he laughed uncontrollably."

- The only time Johnny Most ever missed giving his signature introduction for a broadcast occurred in Dallas in 1986. Ordway recalled the specifics:

  "Johnny decided to sneak out into a back hallway of Reunion Arena to have a smoke. Two cops spotted Most and started threatening to arrest him for smoking a cigarette in a public building. Naturally, Johnny became incensed and started a heated argument with them. Finally, Mavs public relations director Kevin Sullivan was able to smooth things over. By the time Johnny arrived at our broadcasting position, the game was well underway.

  "I asked Johnny on the air why he was 'detained.' He was still irate, so he decided to tell the audience just how ridiculous the police had been. 'Two Dallas cops threatened to arrest me for smoking in the stadium,' he explained. 'Right now in Dallas there are 6,346 robberies taking place, 243 stabbings and shootings are being reported and there's probably a dozen rapes going on. And here's these two cops who think Johnny Most having a cigarette makes me Public Enemy Number One.'"

- Perhaps Celtics fans' favorite Johnny Most call occurred when the Celtics were playing a Yugoslavian team in the McDonald's Classic held in Madrid in 1988. Almost every Yugoslavian player had a long, multi-syllabic name. Johnny knew right from the start, he wouldn't be able to pronounce the players' names correctly. He decided to improvise.

  "Oh, boy," he told his audience, "I'm going to have a little trouble with the names at first. ...Now quickly it goes to the big guy, and now to the lefty, ah, Abrodovich. ...He lost the ball...but it's picked up by the little fellow. ...Oh, I'm having trouble with the names. ...Now the rebound goes to one of the big guys who gets the ball out to one of the little guards, Abrodovich. And...they lost the ball."

  But Johnny's sense of humor came through. "I wish just one of these Yugoslavians was named 'Smith' or Jones,'" he said.

Celtics legend Larry Bird presents Johnny Most with a framed piece of the parquet floor during the ceremony to say goodbye to the Boston Garden fans. © Steve Lipofsky

You can bet Johnny Most was yelling in disbelief about the call that Red Auerbach is questioning. Pictorial Parade/Getty Images

The Zebra-Striped Villains

7here were times when Johnny believed the Celtics were playing against two evil forces—the opposing team and, very definitely, the officials.

Boston—if you were paying the slightest attention—never got a break from the refs. Celtic players would get "slammed," "bloodied," "mauled," "ripped," "attacked," and "cross-body blocked" by the opposition. What really galled Johnny was that the officials would proceed to ignore all of these unprovoked, vicious acts. Young fans, listening to the game on their transistor radios while tucked in bed, just knew Johnny was absolutely correct.

Sometimes Most would even give his audience the impression that the Celtics were perhaps the victims of a dark, sinister conspiracy between the opposition and the heartless men who were making the calls.

Johnny's whole career can be summed up by one of his blistering remarks, "I can't understand these calls. I really can't."

Right or wrong, if a call was against his beloved Celtics, Johnny Most was incensed. In his eyes, the Celtics could do no wrong. Both photos © Steve Lipofsky

Boston great M.L. Carr says farewell to Johnny Most at his retirement dinner in 1990.
© Steve Lipofsky

Johnny's Farewell
to the Celtics and Their Fans
December 3, 1990

In an emotional speech at Boston Garden prior to his microphone being retired, Johnny Most spoke from the heart. He talked about the '53-'54 players, who had made him feel so at home. He thanked the late Walter Brown, the Celtics founder, and Red Auerbach for teaching him about the meaning of friendship and loyalty. Then he addressed the fans, who had faithfully tuned in to listen to his broadcasts for 37 years. "I'll never forget you, and I hope you'll never forget me," he said. "This is not goodbye; it's auf Wiedersehen (until we meet again)."

The occasion prompted a number of letters from ordinary fans and close friends alike.

Former Celtics ballboy Brian Wallace, an author, sent a poem to Johnny:

High Above Courtside

He sits high above courtside in no man's land,
An ever present coffee and a mike in one hand.

From Roughhouse Rudy LaRusso to Big Wayne the Wall
He has seen, called and nicknamed them all.

From Philly to New York and out to LA
76ers, Knick and Laker fans just wish he'd go away.

But for 36 years he's remained in one place
Screaming things like "Russell just put it back in Wilt's face."

He sits here tonight looking so calm
Dying to yell out, "Barkley almost took off Bird's arm."

He sees only one color, of course, which is green
He's called plays at the Garden which he's only seen.

Once labeled by Johnny that nickname you marry
From Jarrin' John to Wide Clyde to Leapin' Larry.

But the thing I remember the Most about John
Was a warm March night in an era long gone.

The leprachaun on the rim was smiling and alive
When the ball hit the wire, the seconds were five.

The Celtics were in trouble, their crown was about to fall
As Greer inbounded Oh, my God, "Havlicek stole the ball."

Johnny Havlicek stole the ball, "It's all over" screamed Most
A play of which Celtic fans to this day still boast.

So from KC to Satch and Jungle Jim, too
We say thank you, Johnny, Boston loses you.
(from the book, *Born Down on A Street*)

Johnny, however, wasn't the retiring type. Despite failing health, he, along with close friend Jim Tuberosa, hosted a talk show in 1992. Even after his legs were amputated due to poor blood circulation, Johnny recovered and continued his broadcasts for two more months. Then Most decided to take "a vacation."

Sadly, on January 3, 1993, Johnny passed away. His calls, his impish personality, his love for the Boston Celtics keep his memory alive in the minds and hearts of New England fans.

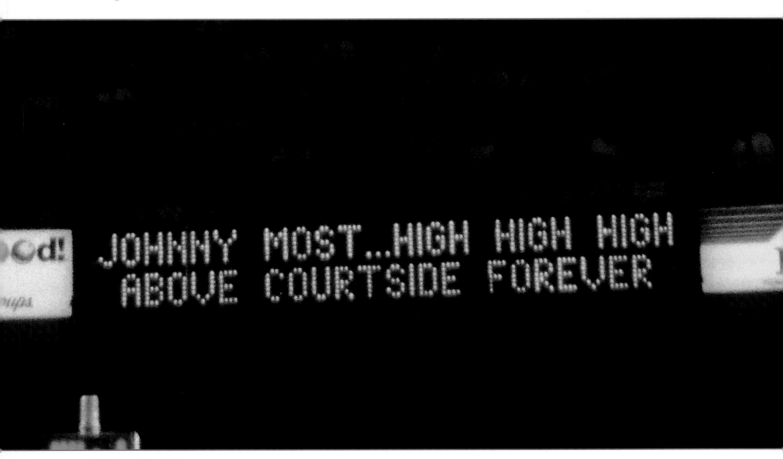

© Steve Lipofsky

The Fans' Guide to Johnny's Nicknames

The Enemy

Ken Regan/NBAE/Getty Images

The Stilt

"I used that expression every time Wilt Chamberlain could hear me because I knew it was a nickname he detested. I didn't coin the phrase, but I 'borrowed' it often because I loved to irritate him." One time Chamberlain complained to the officials about a non-call. "(Bill) Russell didn't try to outmuscle Wilt. That would have been an impossibility. Still, Wilt would constantly moan about Russ fouling him. Once, after he threw a tantrum, I said, 'Poor Wilt. At 7'2" and 280 pounds, he's complaining about all his little bumps and bruises. Please, someone go get him some Gerber's baby food and a pacifier.'"

Jim Cummins/NBAE/Getty Images

The Hatchet Brothers
Philadelphia forwards Steve Mix and Bobby Jones (24) were known as
"The Hatchet Brothers." Johnny said, "I never had a physical confrontation with a
player, but Mix once purposely whacked me on the back of my leg with his travel
bag as he was walking out of Boston Garden."

© Steve Lipofsky

The Great Sir Charles

"The refs give him every call because he's the great Sir Charles," Johnny claimed.
"There's no doubt in my mind that (Charles) Barkley is treated by the refs
as if he were NBA royalty. They favor him because he's only 6'4" and has great
athletic ability. ...He absolutely gets away with murder when he's matched
up against a guy like McHale or Bird."

AP/WWP

The Suit

Johnny was not above taking a few pot shots at the Lakers' "Showtime" atmosphere. He particularly enjoyed chastising coach Pat Riley's passion for fashion. Most would talk about Riley's Hollywood image, his slicked back hair, and his $1,000 suits. Instead of using the LA coach's name, Most would say, "Oh, what a shame. 'The Suit' didn't like that call."

AP/WWP

Little Lord Fauntleroy

"I gave this nickname to Isiah Thomas. 'Little Lord Fauntleroy' was a fictional character, a youngster who was always polite, always mannerly, always cheerful. In other words, Lord Fauntleroy was too good to be true. Thomas reminds me of that kid," said Most. "When Thomas talks to the media, he's always so soft-spoken, acting so shy and humble. And always manages to display that phony little grin. He even uses his little routine on the officials. Unfortunately, some of them are conned by him. I've told my audience, 'Don't be fooled by all his so-called charm. He uses all those tricks to hide the fact that he's a dirty player, just like his partner in crime, Bill Laimbeer.'"

Andrew D. Bernstein/NBAE/Getty Images

The Princess

"(Dominique Wilkins) drives to the basket and always complains if he is so much as touched," said Johnny, "so I started mocking his dislike for contact by using that nickname."

The Untouchable

Another pet name for Wilkins.

The Supreme Hot Dog

Whenever Dennis Rodman, the Pistons forward, would play to the crowd or the cameras, Most would say, "The Hot Dog is at it again. Slap a lot of mustard on him. He's going into his clown act."

Cry, Kelly, Cry

Pistons small forward Kelly Tripucka frequently complained about calls, especially when guarding Larry Bird or Kevin McHale. "He's a non-stop whiner," said Johnny on the air. "Go ahead, Cry, Kelly, Cry."

Andrew D. Bernstein/NBAE/Getty Images

Kareem Puff

Johnny's used this taunt on several occasions when Lakers center Kareem Abdul-Jabbar argued that he was fouled by a Celtics defender. "To Kareem, if you dare to touch him, it's a foul," said Most. "Here's an NBA center who acts like he's special, so delicate and fragile. They should put a 'Handle with Care' sign on his jersey."

Andrew D. Bernstein/NBAE/Getty Images

Counterfeit Bill

Johnny detested the constant "flops" of Detroit center Bill Laimbeer. After watching Laimbeer fake taking a charge, Most decided to christen Laimbeer as Counterfeit Bill. "That's one of my favorites because he was such a complete phony and a disgraceful flopper. Even his acting was terrible," Johnny said. "He'd fall down if the opposing player just gave him a dirty look."

McFilthy and McNasty
Johnny used "McFilthy" and "McNasty" interchangeably for Rick Mahorn and Jeff Ruland. Joked Mahorn, "I preferred McNasty, but I'd rather have been called Rick."

The Brat
"(Rick Barry) was a friend off the court but he was on my all-time crybaby list as a player," Most said.

Roughhouse Rudy LaRusso
"One of the worst cheap-shot artists I ever saw. And I told him so," said Most.

The Grabber
Michael Cooper was the Laker defender who was assigned to cover Larry Bird. "He's good at his job," Most admitted. "However, he's constantly holding Bird's arm or grabbing his jersey. The refs could call a foul on him on each Celtics possession. He's clever, though. He knows just how much he can get away with."

Hysterical Harry
Johnny didn't like Philadelphia public address announcer Dave Zinkoff's loud calls whenever a 76ers player scored a basket. Most believed it was interfering with his broadcasts, so when Zinkoff would start yelling out the name of a player, Johnny would sarcastically say, "There goes Hysterical Harry. He's fallen in love with the sound of his own voice again."

Mr. Nasty
Dennis Johnson was "Mr. Nasty" before he became a Celtic. Once Boston acquired the All-Defensive guard, Johnny began simply calling him DJ.

The Butcher
Johnny's nickname for Paul Silas before he was traded to the Celtics was "The Butcher."

The Linebacker
Before coming to the Celtics, Quinn Buckner was dubbed "The Linebacker" by Johnny because the Bucks point guard's physical style was, in Most's words, "more football than basketball...and he's going to hurt somebody out there."

Gentleman Jerry
Believe it or not, Johnny did occasionally have a kind word for an opposition player.
This was a compliment he gave on the air to Laker Jerry West.

The Celtics

1957 Boston Celtics. Andrew D. Bernstein/NBAE/Getty Images

Rapid Robert
One of Johnny's first classics, used to describe Bob Cousy (14)

The Kentucky Colonel
Former UK star Frank Ramsey (23)

Battling Bill
Bill Sharman (21)

Handy Andy
Andy Phillip (17)

Big Bill
Bill Russell (6)

Jungle Jim
Jim Loscutoff (18)

1968 Boston Celtics. NBAP/NBAE/Getty Images

Leapin' Larry
Larry Siegfried (20)

Slippery Sam
Frequently used by Johnny after Sam Jones (24) drove past a defender. Most also would occasionally throw in a "Sudden Sam" when Jones took a pull-up jumper.

The Jones Boys
Johnny's often used this expression when Sam Jones and KC Jones would defend by using a fullcourt press.

Wayne The Wall
"This one was perfect because when Wayne Embry (28) boxed out under the boards, no one got past him," said Most.

Dynamite Don
Don Nelson (19)

Buckshot Bailey
Bailey Howell (18)

Tricky Ricky
Rick Weitzman (26)

The 1973 Boston Celtics. NBA Photo Library/NBAE/Getty Images

High Henry

To this day, Hank Finkel (29) is greeted by Celtics fans by the nickname Johnny gave him. "It's nice to be remembered, to be asked for an autograph. People ask me if I would sign 'High Henry' for them," the former Celtics center said. "It's all thanks to Johnny."

Tall Paul

Paul Silas (35)

Small Paul

Paul Westphal (44)

Jarrin' John, The Bouncing Buckeye from Ohio State

John Havlicek (17)

Big Red

Dave Cowens (18)

The Prune and the Pear

After hearing Johnny criticize his play, Charles Barkley commented that Most was "just an (expletive deleted) old man who knows absolutely nothing about basketball." Later in his career, Barkley became friends with Johnny and even did a humorous imitation of Most's "Sir Charles" call. Barkley also invented his own nickname for Johnny and his partner, Glenn Ordway. "Charles just came up to Glenn and me one day and said, 'Well, look who's here. If it isn't the prune and the pear.' We both cracked up because it was a pretty good line."

Expressions

In His Shirt

When a Celtics player would play particularly tight, tenacious man-to-man defense, Johnny would refer to the Boston player as being "in his opponent's shirt."

From Downtown

While this phrase is often used today to describe a three-point shot, Most initiated the call in the '50s. "Dolph Schayes was a tremendous shooter from 25 to 30 feet away from the basket. He'd take a minimum of three or four of them a game and he'd make a good percentage," said Johnny. "I started saying, 'Schayes...from downtown...it's good.' If there had been a three-point shot back in his playing days, Dolph would have led the league every year. Incidentally, my longtime friend and broadcasting partner, Al Grenert, who coached Saint Anselm's, was the first expert to recommend that both the college and pro games institute the three-point shot. He believed that the three-point shot would enable smaller players to be more of a factor in a game, particularly in crunch time. His idea, which he proposed and campaigned for in the early '60s, was originally scoffed at. Today, the three-point shot is a major offensive weapon and an exciting element of any basketball game."

Wiggles One In

"Cedric Maxwell was a tremendous rebounder and finesse player. He was skinny, quick and deceptively strong," Most said. "He'd go against players who outweighed him and would just find a way to squeeze through the defense and score. "Rather than just say that Cedric scored on a layup, I came up with 'wiggles one in.' I thought it was an effective, quick way of describing Maxwell's efforts."

Dips, Shoots, Good

"Free throws can be boring to a radio audience. A play-by-play announcer can use the time to talk about strategy while a player is shooting foul shots," Most said. "I came up with what I thought was a quick way to describe a free throw attempt. It also gave me an extra second to give the score or talk about the tone of the game. 'Dips, shoots, good'—that's what I came up with."

Fiddles and Diddles

"There are times when a point guard stalls while his team sets up for an offensive play. He might dribble right, then dribble left, then simply hold the ball," Most explained. "There's not much action, so I decided that rather than describe a meaningless five seconds of dribbling, I simply say something like '(Maurice) Cheeks fiddles and diddles.' In the early '80s Mo Cheeks would dribble from side to side while waiting for Moses Malone to position himself near the lane."

Daddles and Doodles

An extension of "fiddles and diddles."

Tricky Dribbles

Johnny first used the phrase in the late '50s when Philadelphia point guard Guy Rodgers would do some fancy but meaningless dribbling while waiting for Wilt Chamberlain to catch up to the play.

Dipsey-Doo

A double-pump layup or an off-balance, underhand scoop shot.

On the Gallop, Gallops

Johnny's terms for a ballhandler on the fastbreak.

Rips the Rebound

Whenever David Cowens went to the boards, he "ripped the rebound," usually with one hand.

Slow-Motion Drive

Johnny's description of a Chris Ford move to the basket.

Bang

Johnny's patented indication of a converted field goal attempt, especially when the shot came from long range.

Stops and Pops or Stops, Pops, Swish

First used by Johnny to describe Jerry West's pull-up jumper.

The Pumpkin

Johnny's term for a Kevin McHale shot, with little spin on the ball.

Tosses Up a Loaf of Bread

Johnny's description of Knicks forward Jerry Lucas's set shot.

Rainbow

A Robert Parish high-arching jumper from 16 feet.

Pulling a Stanislofsky

Stanislofsky was a Russian actor whose acting methods were overdramatic and exaggerated. When Tommy Heinsohn coached the Celtics, he would complain that players who "flopped" to draw charging fouls were "pulling a Stanislofsky." Johnny liked the expression so much, he "borrowed" it for his broadcasts. Johnny's top four floppers: Jerry Sloan, Mike Newlin, Clyde Lee, and KC Jones.

Wing Dinger

A tight game in the final seconds. This phrase was also used by Johnny when he announced greyhound racing at Plainfield Racetrack to describe a photo finish.

Muscle Tussle

Whenever two opposing centers or power forwards were involved in very physical play, Johnny would warn his listeners that things were "getting ugly" by using this term.

© Steve Lipofsky

Andrew D. Bernstein/NBAE/Getty Images

Critical Acclaim for
HIGH ABOVE COURTSIDE:
THE LOST MEMOIRS OF JOHNNY MOST

American Sportscasters Association:
"A must read for all those who remember one of the NBA's most intriguing and affable sportscasters."

Hall of Famer Robert Parish:
"The book brought back great memories for me. No one could give a better insider's look at the Celtics than Johnny Most. He was an NBA legend and anyone who has read *High Above Courtside* knows that Johnny belongs in the Hall of Fame. His classic calls will go down as the greatest in NBA history."

The New York Post's "Insiders" Kevin Kernan and Steve Serby:
"We love this book on legendary Boston announcer Johnny Most … He bled Boston green but he broke in covering the 'Boys of Summer' on the Brooklyn Dodgers Radio Network. There's great stories on every page."

Frommer Sports Syndicate:
"This worthy read belongs in a prominent place on your sports bookshelf."

Jim Donaldson, *Providence Journal*:
"A must read for every Celtics fan!"

Jim Baker, *Boston Herald*:
"A million great Celtic anecdotes … Most's thoughts on Bill Russell were particularly insightful … I recommend it to every basketball fan."

Rick Barry, Hall of Famer and KNBR radio host:
"Johnny Most was the supreme homer. Who cares, though? He was a great broadcaster, an emotional man who could paint vivid verbal pictures for his audience as well as any play-by-play man in the NBA. *High Above Courtside* perfectly captures his personality and shows why he was one of the game's greatest characters."

Hall of Famer Tommy Heinsohn:

"If you want to know what life was like for Johnny Most on a day-to-day basis, read *High Above Courtside*. It's the ultimate insider's look at the Celtics.

Jim Armstrong, *Denver Post*:

"Anyone who enjoys the NBA must read this book."

Hall of Famer Larry Bird:

"There was nothing phony about Johnny Most. *High Above Courtside* isn't just about the Celtics; it's about a great broadcaster who was loved by every Boston player and every New England fan who followed the Celtics. He loved his job and he loved the Celtics. I'm proud to have had him as a friend."

Steve Holman, Atlanta Hawks broadcaster:

"Johnny Most gave me my big break. He gave a lot of young broadcasters encouragement and advice. His 37 years with the Celtics is chronicled perfectly in *High Above Courtside*. …When Johnny was gravely ill, I asked him for permission to use his introduction for my broadcasts. I use it before every Hawks game. It's my tribute to a man whose calls are still classics today."

Hall of Famer Bill Walton:

"There's no better history of the Celtics than *High Above Courtside*. Johnny was there for all 16 Boston Championships. His personal thoughts reflect his tremendous knowledge of the NBA, the Celtics, Red Auerbach, and every player who wore the Celtics uniform. Celtic broadcasters will come and go, but no one will ever replace Johnny Most in the hearts of the fans. *High Above Courtside* tells precisely why he will always be known as the Voice of the Celtics."

Buck Harvey, San Antonio *Express-News*:

"Johnny Most was one of the NBA's true legends. Every coach and player throughout the league, it seems, has a favorite story about the colorful Boston Celtics radio play-by-play announcer, who passed away in 1993. *High Above Courtside* provides hundreds of classic (and sometimes hilarious) moments in this one-of-a-kind broadcasters career. … I found it thoroughly enjoyable."

Celebrate the Heroes of Boston Sports
in These Other Releases from Sports Publishing!

Tales from the Boston College Sideline
by Reid Oslin

- 5.5 x 8.25 hardcover
- 200 pages
- photos throughout
- $19.95
- 2004 release!

Tales from the Patriots Sideline
by Michael Felger

- 5.5 x 8.25 hardcover
- 200 pages
- photos throughout
- $19.95
- 2004 release!

Tom Brady: Most Valuable Patriot
by *The Boston Herald*

- 8.5 x 11 hardcover
- 128 pages
- color photos throughout
- $24.95

Ted Williams: The Pursuit of Perfection
by Bill Nowlin and Jim Prime

- 8.5 x 11 hardcover
- photos throughout
- Includes audio CD!
- 250 pages • $39.95

High Above Courtside: The Lost Memoirs of Johnny Most
by Mike Carey with Jamie Most

- 6 x 9 hardcover
- 425 pages
- eight-page photo section
- $24.95

The Red Sox Encyclopedia: Second Edition
by Robert Redmount

- 8.5 x 11 hardcover
- 320 pages
- 300+ photos throughout
- $39.95

More Tales from the Red Sox Dugout
by Bill Nowlin and Jim Prime

- 5.5 x 8.25 hardcover
- 200 pages
- photos throughout
- $19.95

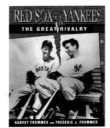

Red Sox vs. Yankees: The Great Rivalry
by Harvey and Frederic Frommer

- 8.5 x 11 hardcover
- 256 pages
- color photos throughout
- $24.95 • 2004 release!

Tales from the Boston Bruins
by Kerry Keene

- 5.5 x 8.25 hardcover
- 200 pages
- photos throughout
- $19.95

New England Patriots: 2004 Super Bowl Champions
by *The Boston Herald*

- 8.5 x 11 hardcover and softcover • 160 pages
- color photos throughout
- $29.95 (hardcover)
- $19.95 (softcover)

To order at any time, please call toll-free **877-424-BOOK (2665)**.
For fast service and quick delivery, order on-line at **www.SportsPublishingLLC.com**.